THE LAST LABYRINTH

ARUN JOSHI

Orient Paperbacks
DELHI | MUMBAI | HYDERABAD

For
Arjun, Nihar and Shonar.

www.orientpaperbacks.com

ISBN : 978-81-222-0506-0

New edition 2012

The Last Labyrinth

Cover design by Vision Studio

Published by
Orient Paperbacks
(A division of Vision Books Pvt. Ltd.)
5A/8 Ansari Road, New Delhi-110 002

Printed in India at
Saurabh Printers Pvt. Ltd., Noida

Cover Printed at
Ravindra Printing Press, Delhi-110 006

ARUN JOSHI (1939-1993), son of a botanist and an eminent educationist, was born in Varanasi and educated in India and the U.S. After getting his Masters degree in Industrial Management from M.I.T., he returned to India to pursue a career in the corporate world.

Yet writing remained his passion. In the five novels he wrote he spun out some of the most thought-provoking and outstanding fiction written in the twentieth century Indian literature and firmly established his credentials as a writer of rare talent and sensitivity. 'I seek a belief and a faith beyond psychology', he said. His search was essentially spiritual. He explored lives as labyrinth — hopeless mazes where one may get irretrievably lost or discover the shining secret at the core of life.

Although English remained his 'own first language' he was equally an admirer of Hindi poetry of Dinkar, Ageya, Sumitranandan Pant and Nirala. *The Last Labyrinth* won him the Sahitya Akademi Award, India's highest literary honour in 1982.

~

'*The Last Labyrinth* is considered an outstanding contribution to Indian English literature for its restless search for a meaning in human existence, its treatment of the multiple levels of reality, challenging narrative technique and an evocative use of language.'

Sahitya Akademi Award Citation

LIBRARY OF SOUTH ASIAN LITERATURE

Library of South Asian Literature is an ongoing endeavour to publish in English an eclectic selection of some of the finest writings from the rich diversity of South Asian Literature. It attempts to bring together books regarded as landmarks in their language, for having won literary awards or critical acclaim, or having been a major influence in their genre, creating a new narrative style or simply representing an outstanding writer's art.

Readers are invited to recommend books to make this more truly representative of the vigorous literary tradition of South Asia. These maybe sent by mail, fax or email to Editor, Orient Paperbacks, 5A/8, Ansari Road, New Delhi-110 002. Tel: +91-11-2327 8877, 2327 8878 Fax: +91-11-2327 8879, email: mail@orientpaperbacks.com

PART ONE

1

Above all, I have a score to settle. I forget nothing, forgive no one.

It is two in the morning. An hour to go. Geeta sleeps next door. Banjo outside the gate. Banjo is not asleep after all. I can hear him working at the sand. Phut, phut, phut. That is his hang-up. Beyond Banjo is more sand. Beyond the sand is the sea, washing at the far end the shores of another continent.

Why is the sea so grey here? It is blue down in Goa and bluer still on the coast of Ceylon (now, Sri Lanka). They have a city by her name over there. Anuradhapura. A city of ruins. I was sent there once by my father — to negotiate deals. I tried to know the prices of things, the structure of discounts. They only talked of Nirvana and that other visitor, the Royal Bhikku, Mahinda, Ashoka's messenger, and how when he spoke in King Tissa's Court the Emperor wept. So did the courtiers. The Sakyamuni, the Tathagata, still lived among them, I was told, which meant some one had beat me to the contract. I couldn't care less. I drank all the way back thinking of what I had read on a board beside a spiky monument. 'There are beings who perish through not knowing the Dhamma' said the battered board. 'Go Ye forth, O Bhikkus, and proclaim the Dhamma. There will be some who will understand...' Flying past Madurai I thought yes, there must be *some, somewhere,* who understood. But where? And, giving up, I drank all the more. At Santa Cruz, amidst the din of the customs, my father said, 'You should not have drunk so much. What after all is a contract?'

'It is not the contract,' I said.

'What is it then?'

I told him.

He put his hand on my shoulder and looked into my eyes, his face flushed with emotion and embarrassment. A week later he was dead, of a heart attack, between four and five in the morning, according to K.

I was twenty five and a millionaire.

~

This illness has turned many things topsy turvy. One thing badly turvy is my sleep routine. Three to ten in the morning and four to six in the afternoon. There is nothing that K has not tried. Sleeping pills, tranquillisers, warm baths. But three to ten it remains and four to six. He is puzzled. I can see that. Your blood is only chemicals now, he says, pure unmanageable chemicals. Your body is God's chariot, says Tuka Ram. There you are!

Chemicals or no chemicals, I have become a nuisance. To K, to Geeta, to myself. No doubt about that. Geeta sits with me until midnight. I tell her then to go. From midnight till three I sit and moon. If I believed in God I could pray, maybe run a rosary through my fingers. But that's out. Sitting around, I get into arguments: with the living and with the dead, with myself. And I have had enough of the world's arguments. To shut everyone up, I took one night to this minute-book. Which night? Why this book? A tale hangs by this minute-book. Another by this cottage. There is nothing a tale doesn't hang by.

I fool around in this book like a clown performing before a looking glass. I get into arguments nonetheless. I shall sleep better when our brief winter sets in. To judge by the ocean breeze it should be round the corner.

The earth turning slowly around the sun. 1000 miles a minute. Moon around the earth. Stars and spacemen. Villagers of Srikakulam gone gay with songs from the Satellite. Hunger of the body. Hunger of the spirit. You suffer from one or the other, or both.

2

That summer in Delhi, the summer of Anuradha, I was thirty five. Still a millionaire. Many times over. I had been married to an extraordinary woman. I had two children. That was the way the cards were stacked that summer evening when, more or less drunk, amidst the detonation of moths, we sat near the swimming pool of the Intercontinental Hotel. There was in the air a perfume of *motia*, and the prelanding whine of planes. Beyond them all, audible only to my ear, a grey cry threshed the night air: I want. I want. I want. Through the light of my days and the blackness of my nights and the disquiet of those sleepless hours beside my wife, within reach of the tranquillisers, I had sung the same strident song: I want. I want. I want. I want.

I had been to the world's finest universities, or what were supposed to be such. According to Mr. Thapar, who kept account of such things, a quarter million had been spent on my education. And there were things that I had picked up by myself. I knew that money was dirt, a whore. So were houses, cars, carpets. I knew of Krishna, of the lines he had spoken: of Buddha at Sarnath, under the full moon of July, setting in motion the wheel of Righteousness; of Pascal, on whom I did a paper at Harvard: 'Let us weigh the gain and loss in wagering that God is, let us estimate these two chances. If you gain, you gain all, if you lose, you lose nothing.' All this I knew and much else. And yet, at the age of thirty five, I could do no better than produce the same rusty cry: I want. I want.

I had learnt another thing, one among the several cadenzas, simple and complex, with which I conducted my orchestras of discontent: I had learnt to corner companies. And, that summer evening by the swimming pool of the Intercontinental, amidst the drinks and the eats, while a tape of Begum Akhtar spilled out her unhappy songs and, unknown to me, Aftab set sail for distant seas, that evening I had already laid the pincers on Aftab's business.

There is the memory of a warm Delhi night. Inside the great hotel Aftab, goggled, in a maroon jacket, had held a reception for the Plastic Manufacturers Association. I had come only to talk of business. I was in a hurry. I was always in a hurry then, like a hare chased by unseen hounds. I had noticed Anuradha like one notices a monument: tall, handsome, ruined. We stared across a dozen glossy heads. Her eyes, just a little slanted, had that inky blackness that files the eyes of the victims of small pox. She might have been thirty, thirty-five. She could have been from Bengal, from Sikkim, from the valleys of Nepal. She did not look clever. She wore costumes of twenty years ago — brocade sari, large gold borders, sleeves up to the elbow, antique jewellery. She was obsolete like her husband.

Later, I invited them for drinks — I was not yet finished with my manoeuvres. The open air, the chit-chat of tourists, the twilight, quietened my nerves. Aftab did not drink. It was Anuradha who kept me company. Aftab smoked his hand rolled cigarettes, filled with heaven knew what. He laughed easily. The dim lighting had turned him into a pale prince.

'Aftab Rai is a rather peculiar person,' Mr. Thapar had briefed me. He was apologetic as though in some way he had a hand in creating him. 'You will have to be patient with him. His wife is more balanced that way. Perhaps, you can work through her.' What made him think I worked through anyone? I had my vanity about my forthrightness.

'Who is he anyway?'

'His great-grand-father was a zamindar, a courtier of Wajid Ali Shah. They fled to Benaras after the mutiny. They have lived there for more than a hundred years.'

'That is a hell of a long time. Anything else?'

'Not much. He is a secretive sort of a man.'

'And the wife?'

'I am afraid not much is known about her. She was a film star for a short while. Very briefly, though.'

'I never heard of her,' I said.

'You must have been in America at the time. She retired after her marriage.'

'Who runs the company?'

'No one really knows. His wife has a reputation for being clever, shrewd.'

I looked at her now. She, too, had been transformed by the lighting. It had levelled the pits in her face, brought out the unquenched fires that constantly burnt in those haunted eyes. Even her antique costume had come alive. It lent her a personality very different from any I had ever known. She was attractive; I had to hand it to her. Alone with me for a moment while Aftab hunted for an ashtray, Anuradha said, 'A Bhaskar, what is a Bhaskar doing in business?'

I stared at her. There was a tattoo mark on her forehead, a permanent bindi burnt into the skin.

'What should a Bhaskar be doing?' I snapped.

'You are a Brahmin,' she said as though it explained everything.

I wondered why her question had angered me.

She kept quiet, wanting, perhaps, not to annoy me. But I would not let her be.

'Not everyone has the brains to run a business, you know.'

I saw the shot go home. She averted her eyes, took out a cigarette. I offered her a light. She cupped the flame warding it from the draft. I noticed, then, the tracery of *mehndi* on her pink palms. A little hot wave, tinged with sorrow, travelled down my spine. The delicate curlicues, golden arabesques, road signs of fate, wound and unwound, turned upon themselves. I had seen that hand before: as a child, as a boy, in my fantasies of lust. I stared at her not quite understanding what was happening to me. At thirty five, I was a worn-out weary man incapable of spontaneous feeling. What, then, was this?

Aftab came back. 'I am going to the dargah tonight,' he announced. 'Come with me.'

He addressed us as though Anuradha was as much of a stranger as I. But there was warmth in his invitation, a charm that could not be spurned. I said I would come.

~

Through lanes paved with shadows, Aftab led the way. We, the actress and the tycoon, followed. The alcohol weighed me down, but my mind was restless again, full of frustration. Another evening wasted; the attack parried.

It was late. The moonlight had tinged everything a light blue. White-robed faceless figures moved silently through the lanes. From a balcony, amidst the giggling of women, the notes of a sarangi floated down. These were narrow lanes meant only for walking. The houses were old with low roofs and stoops across the gutter. Alleys shot off in all directions. Barefoot boys rushed out of them, quiet as cats. A donkey stood tied to a stake. I was reminded of the old section of Cairo.

'What on earth are we going to the dargah for?' I asked Anuradha.

'Why did you come?'

I shrugged. 'I wish I were in bed.'

'The walk may help you sleep better.'

'Nothing can help me sleep better.'

Out in the open, her voice had changed. It was resonant, yet hushed, as though it came from afar.

'I am told you were in the movies.' I put it as though it were an abuse.

'Who told you?'

'I have my informants.'

'Mr. Thapar?'

I was surprised she should know about Mr. Thapar.

'Well, what do you have against Mr. Thapar?'

'Why should I have anything against him?'

The softness was gone. She smiled but her smile had an abrasive edge. I hardened. So, a little later, did she. And so did the core of the night. She wrapped her sari tightly around her, receding into herself. My steps sounded loud on the pavement, loud and obscene, footsteps of an interloper.

Under a clump of trees, nearly one with the shadows, Aftab waited. He looked back towards us, then looked away. When I was within range I could hear him softly calling. 'Amjad Mian. Amjad Mian.'

'Aftab Rai?' a voice called back. Then an old man stepped out of the dark cavities of the wall, an old man with a beard, holding a lantern. The two of them exchanged greetings, quietly, in great politeness, showing neither surprise nor pleasure.

Through a narrow entrance, they led the way into the dargah itself. First look, and I knew it was a mistake. There was nothing I loathed more than I loathed the sight of death and here, amidst the cenotaphs and the gravestones, there was death with a vengeance. I felt tricked. To be shifted so suddenly from the euphoric heights of the Intercontinental to these desolate mounds was a rebuke I did not deserve. Anuradha's sari brushed against my arm. Aftab approached us looking, more or less, a ghost.

'My friend will like to tell you something about this dargah,' he declared, addressing no one in particular.

Amjad Mian was no guide. But he liked to talk, considered it probably his duty, like old Leela, to educate, reform. White-haired, eyes receded beyond visibility, draped in black, he addressed us from his stony perch. My attention kept wandering but was pulled back again and again to his melancholy drone. Bustami banished from Baghdad. Mansur Hallaj put to death raving to the end. Ana'l Haq,

Ana'l Haq, I am God. Next came the Chishtis, said Amjad Mian. Khwaja Mu'inuddin wandering into India before the invasions of the Ghor, wandering on into the realms of the Hindu Prithvi Raj. 'Alone, hungry, his feet bitten with the sands of Rajputana,' cried Amjad Mian, moved at the vision. 'Alone, without imperial power at his back, the Khwaja was no less a success in Ajmer, Aftab Sahib, no less a success.' Aftab Sahib nodded several times. I thought of the failure of my business mission. Khwaja Qutbuddin Bakhtiar Kaki dying in ecstasy while singers sang:

Kushtagane khanjare taslim ra,
Har zaman as ghaib digar ast.

Breaking his silence, Aftab translated for us: 'When the dagger of submission has killed you, there will come new lives from unseen worlds.'

Unseen worlds..... Unseen worlds. Everyone looking for unseen worlds.

Khwaja Mu'inuddin Bakhtiar Kaki. Baba Farid. Iltutmish, the king. Wanters all. Sheikh Nizamuddin himself, Mehboob-i-Ilahi, in whose dargah we stood. What did he have to say about unseen worlds?

'He saw seven kings,' said Amjad Mian. 'Seven filled the throne of Delhi, then went.'

'Went where?' I teased.

'Where we all have to go,' said Amjad Mian profoundly.

Nevertheless, here was food for thought. To have had royal esteem, commanded the hearts of men, seen the play of the Khiljis and the Tughlaqs and have remained uninvolved, unmoved, that must have been trial enough.

'Each sultan, on bended knee, begged him to visit. Not once, sir, not once did he visit the durbar of the seven kings. Not once.'

Anuradha listened with hands on one hip. Her face was expressionless. It struck me then that there was something that those three knew that I did not. Tired, I sat down. Amjad Mian carried on, addressing the gravestones. *Tariqat, Haqiqat, Tawakkul, Sabr, Khauf, Ishq, Rida, Fana.* Much else. He was a learned man. But how was one to acquire all those virtues?

'*Fana,*' he cried. '*Fana.* The body must first die.'

I lit a cigarette but was told sharply to put it out. I put it out. Amjad Mian had his prerogatives. But if the Aulia could introduce music, at the cost even of inquisitions, why couldn't Amjad Mian let me smoke? I was too tired to argue. There was silence. Amjad Mian looked at me with suspicion. The rebuke had momentarily nipped the flow of his rhetoric.

'Shall we see some more of the dargah?' Aftab said at last.

I wanted to say: Hell with your dargah.

'I am not going any further,' I said.

'Are you tired?' drawled Aftab.

'Of Mr. Nizamuddin and his friends, yes.'

He let out a little sigh which, I came to realize, signified a laugh, a sob, a smirk, from some other world. 'Anuradha will keep you company,' he said.

After they were gone, Anuradha said, 'You can smoke now.' I lit a cigarette, thinking of K at my father's funeral. My mind wandered touching on stray irrelevant images: the banks of the Ganga at Haridwar where I stood clasping the urn of my father's ashes; the odd stranger in the hospital, the messenger of Shani, who had somehow slipped into my room that Saturday morning and whom I had refused a coin and whose curse I still carried; Geeta in the study with her brother's commandant, silently crying; my mother's room and the stain of acetone. From that stain on the carpet it flew to the woman who had been left behind to keep me company. My eyes travelled up from her feet and thigh and belly — she had a fine figure — to her face. She was looking down at me, serious, speculative, her black eyes blacker.

'Sit down,' I said.

She did not sit down.

There was a silence broken by the prolonged whistling of a locomotive. On the heels of the whistle, quite out of the blue, she said, 'You are here to grab his business, aren't you?'

I looked up sharply. Her face was in shadow but the eyes stood out. She looked only worried.

'I don't *grab* anything,' I said.

'You can give it any name you like but isn't it his business that you are after?'

'What if I am?'

'He does not know about it.'

'Shall I inform him?'

I could not help a laugh. I was at last getting a rise out of them, getting a handle on them.

'I wish you would leave him alone,' she said.

'Why?'

'Because he is no match for you. And...'

'Yes?'

'In a way, you are no match for him.'

'No?' She took a couple of steps and sat down next to me. I could smell her perfume. The locomotive hooted some more and let out steam. Sound travelled far at that hour. Her face was no longer in shadow. She had the features of women one saw in Moghul miniatures. I was fascinated.

'There is another reason,' she said.

'Reason for what?'

'Why you should leave him alone.'

I waited, turning the cigarette in my fingers.

'I don't think it is his business that you want.'

'No?'

'No. I don't know what you want,' she went on, indifferent to my little barbs, 'but it is not his business.'

'You sound like Mr. Thapar.'

'Please don't make fun of me.'

Those words of Anuradha — words that, no doubt, were also a warning — I failed to hear them in the dargah's deafening silence. Instead, I thought I would bend the moment to my advantage. I thought I would explain to her how things stood and get her on my side. In the battlefield that I believed the world to be there were always sides, yours and the other man's, and you had to break them loose from the other man's side and bring them to your own before you could launch the final blow.

I told her then, in my special brand of candour and cunning, how it was in Aftab's interest to hand me his business; how he was neither suited for it nor did he seem much interested; how he could do so much more with the cash that he would get. And, finally, I gave her the most formidable argument of them all. In business, as elsewhere, I told her, it was the survival of the fittest.

'He is not organized enough to survive,' I said.

In reply, she put her hand on my arm. A strand of her hair had come loose and she was laughing.

'You take yourself so seriously,' she said.

I felt rage whipping at the end of my spine and shooting up to the skull, to some dark hollows where the serpents slept, just waiting to be stirred. But her hand was there on my arm. How was I to push it away? What was I to do with it? She had said what she had set out to say. Her laughter, too, had ended. And yet the hand was there, light and soft, transmitting its perfumed warmth. There was a solitaire on the second finger. A moon-beam broke on it: violet, orange, and blue. The fire started to subside. The snakes continued to sleep. I thought of the *mehndi* on her palm.

'I saw *mehndi* on your hands,' I said.

She took a while to understand.

'Oh.' And, releasing my arm, she looked at her hands. 'I have been to a wedding,' she said. 'Why?'

She had long tapering fingers. There were glass bangles on her wrist. I wanted to hold that hand. Inflamed with sudden desire, I felt absurd amidst that procession of tombstones. The feeling passed.

Aftab's soft voice approached in the distance. Amjad Mian stood before us and looked down, from me to Anuradha and back. I could not see his eyes.

'I am going back to the hotel,' I told Aftab.

'Where is the hurry?'

'I need to sleep.'

He looked at Anuradha, then at me. 'We shall drop you, then,' he said.

~

I stood in my room, high above the city of Delhi. I had been undressing. What had thrown me off was Anuradha's perfume on my arm. It was a peculiar perfume, something I had never come across. There was *raat-ki-raani* in it and a touch of summer earth after rain. But there was something else as well, something rare and dense, something that might have been known only to Scheherzade and the seraglios of the Moghul. It was fine, exotic stuff meant to lift one's spirits. Why, then, did it make me sad?

I looked at myself in the mirror: lean, crow-footed, greying. I could not, then, see the hunger but there was the boredom and the fed-up-ness, endless depths of it.

That evening was a failure, an unmistakable defeat. Survival of the fittest made no sense to her as it had ceased to make sense to my father.

I awoke in the middle of the night, depressed, the taste of tranquillisers in my mouth. My first thought was of Anuradha. I thought of her as she had been in the dargah, sitting close to me, her hand on my arm. And I also thought of the moves I still had to make to capture Aftab's business.

Visit us in Benaras, Aftab had said. I knew I would have to. My business with him was not yet over.

3

How far I have travelled from that morning I took over my first plant. We went to the Elephanta Caves that morning, my father and I. In the evening we walked this beach. To my left, diagonally across the window, I can see the mound, where honeymooning couples pose for photographs, and where my father had stood that evening struggling with words. Was it the visit to Elephanta that had turned him on? Or, was it a deeper turbulence?

'Let us keep the launch to ourselves,' he had said. It was a mild morning. Tourists crowded the Gateway, taking pictures. As we sped through the Colaba harbour he pointed out the different ships. There was Vikrant, the aircraft carrier, with no sign of the aircraft. Sailors, polishing the cannon of a frigate, waved to us as we went past. My father waved back. We made a detour because he wanted to look at the reactor at Trombay. As we approached the great phallic dome we fell silent.

Crossing the pier at Elephanta my father said to K who also accompanied us, 'The first time I came here was when I learnt Som's mother had cancer.' K looked guilty as though he had personally been responsible for my mother's death.

I thought of them, my parents, one tall the other short, getting off the boat in silence. How did they cross the pier? In silence? Small talk? Laughter? Did they hold hands? It meant the same thing: that time was running out. I must have been fourteen at the time. Men came from the city, from the factories, even from distant towns, professional cheer-uppers. My father did not prohibit them. He sat quietly, patiently, a lock of grey hair on his forehead, listening to their drivel, his mind in fever. Only K knew of its total confusion. It was to him that my father made those absurd suggestions. Lung transplant was one of them, using his own lung. Exasperated, one day K had shouted back at him, 'Don't be ridiculous. Throw out all those gods and goddesses and she might have a chance.'

On the island of Elephanta we sat on a bench in a grove of tamarind. My father plucked a fern and chewed upon it and watched a trio of ratings walk by, in step, in spite of themselves. Waving the fern he said. 'Of late, you know, I have been wondering about causes. Causes of things, things that happen to men, to objects.' His comment was addressed to neither of us in particular. He did not continue. We moved on to the great cave, cooler and darker than the groves of tamarind.

We stared at the Trimurti: heavy lipped Brahma; Rudra with snakes and a third eye; Vishnu almost effeminate. Probably, the same troubadour in different garbs, sent to foul up men's understanding. Coming out, on the edge of a cliff, we met the ratings again. My father fell into conversation with them. They were dark, full of laughter, respectful. They came from the Vikrant where they worked on the planes. 'You fly them?' my father said excitedly. They were embarrassed. They were mechanics as anyone, except my father, could see. 'Never mind,' he said. 'You will fly them one day.' He explained to them the history of the caves and the geology of the island on which we stood. He pointed out to them the Buddhist burial mounds. He was a master of such things. On parting, smiling shyly, the ratings gave him a picture of Christ. It changed colour when he shifted it in his hands.

4

I have had a tiff with Mr. Thapar and another with Geeta. They cannot understand why I hate her so but, then, nor do they know how desperately I had once loved her and, in the terrible loneliness of my heart still do. They know I had something to do with her and they think they know all. But what do they know of thoughts and sensations that no words can capture, that would burn the very paper they are written on? What do they know of the Anuradha that I knew, or of Gargi, or of Lal Haveli, that sepulchral, sensual den of Aftab's amidst the labyrinths of Benaras.

Even my dreams are not free of them. Strange murky shapes float through their tangled web. Animals and wheels of fire and brilliant suns blazing away in dark starless skies. I see myself grotesque, naked, my face distorted as if in a funny mirror. Anuradha, my poor Anuradha, walking shoeless across a burning desert. Gargi sitting in the middle of nowhere reading a book, throwing a *cowrie* shell, and saying to me: 'She is your *shakti*.'

At times, my mother takes Gargi's place. 'Don't,' she cries, 'don't,' as my arm sweeps across a tableful of gods.

~

The peon came to the dormitory one morning and led me through sun-drenched corridors, holding me by the hand, even though I was fifteen. I knew she was dead. We went to the quarters of the Housemaster. The Housemaster looked very solemn and also held my hand.

It was winter. I was dressed for athletics. The peon, the Housemaster and I, spiked shoes and all, went to the Headmaster's house. In single file. There was a grove of guavas in the Headmaster's yard and I remember the sharp smell of ripening guavas. The Headmaster sat on the verandah in his dressing gown, reading a newspaper. He peered at us from above the rims of his glasses. That was his habit even though he was quite young. Then he called for his wife. All four of us sat in a circle in cane chairs, the peon stood at the back.

'I have bad news for you, Bhaskar,' the Headmaster said.

I started to cry. The Headmaster said, 'Your father has suggested that you don't come for the funeral.'

The Headmaster's wife led me inside and gave me hot milk and cream biscuits. It was a ritual of sorrow. She stood watching as I sipped the milk. She was a young woman, firm and shapely. She wore a night dress over which she had thrown a dressing gown. Arms folded, she stood watching me through soft warm eyes. I lifted my gaze from the floor and looked at her, begging her to explain the meaning of it all. She stepped forward, close enough so that I could smell the sleep filled odour of her body. She passed her hand through my hair, starting from the forehead and going all the way to the nape of the neck. She, too, had probably been to a wedding and there was *mehndi* on her palm. And while she pushed the hair away from my forehead I was mesmerized by these hieroglyphs of a new world, a world of wild erotic instincts. That night as I lay in the dormitory I had thought not of my dead mother but the Headmaster's wife. I went back to her next day to request her to persuade her husband to let me go home for a few days. My mother's funeral was over but I wanted to meet my father. 'Must you go?' she said, searching my face.

I nodded, keeping back, not tears but a great roaring hollowness. 'I understand,' she said, 'I shall speak to my husband.'

'Thank you,' I said. 'Thank you.'

My father stood in the airport lobby, dapper as ever, arms at the back, talking to Mr. Thapar. Mr. Thapar noticed me; my father did not. When he did, he came forward, brisk and businesslike. He shook my hand. He said, 'I did not want to disturb your studies.' He looked into my eyes and, perhaps, saw what the Headmaster's wife had seen and put his arm around me. We drove to the cottage where she had spent her last days. There were mourners on the patio. Mr. Thapar took care of them. My father and I went to her room. It gave out her perfume as it had always done. We stood on opposite sides of the bed, totally unable to communicate. Then he moved to my side. I was fifteen but nearly as tall as him. He put his hands on my shoulders. I thought he was going to embrace me. But he simply clutched at my shoulders kneading them with a jerky desperate motion that I did not understand. I looked into his face and saw the uncontrollable trembling of the mouth. Tears rolled down his face. His chest heaved with muffled sobs as the chests of grown men do when they cry. I saw his tears and the heaving of his chest but I did not cry. Behind my eyes, and in the cavities of my skull, the same strange hollowness roared endlessly.

~

Seven years later, coming back from Elephanta, walking on this beach, my father brooded. Of late, he had often been like that. Long silences interrupted by momentary elation. K watched him warily. As dusk fell and the sky darkened, the storm over my father's brooding broke. His hair blowing in the breeze he said, 'I believe in science, yes, but science cannot solve the problem of the causes. Not many realize this paradox. We assume that the immediate stimulus to an occurrence is its cause, don't we?' He looked at me. 'There are processes in our plant that use certain methods for providing heat. But the same heat could be provided by totally different means. Theoretically, you could concentrate the light of the sun, or even of a star that died a million years ago, and actuate some of our processes. Or, you could say that the scientist who developed the process is the cause, or the workers, or Thapar or I. Or, maybe, my mother who bore me or *her* father. You see how complicated it gets... Then there are causes behind causes, especially periods... So, you see, I have been wondering...'

He fell abruptly silent and blushed like a boy caught in a prohibited act. At another time he might have broken off at this point. But whatever it was, he had it badly on his mind. 'You see,' he began, 'you see, I have been wondering if there couldn't possibly be a First Cause.'

He fell silent again. The three of us walked up and down the deserted beach. In the sky above stars had begun to come out. He started again.

'Have you noticed the fundamental unity in the construction of the universe, K? Great galaxies oscillate, so does the minutest particle of quartz. It is the same cell that is the building block of every living animal. Everything happens in cycles. Birth, Growth, Decline and Death. Couldn't there be a First Cause that would explain everything, whose nature might lie behind the natures of all the rest? I spoke of heat. All light could have a First Cause too. So could all sound. So could all love. Hate. Anger. They, too, are energies, aren't they?' He looked around, a little uncertain, at the empty beach, at the dark sea, then carried on defiantly. 'Of course, they are. So is all thought. The mystics say as much.'

'But what is the evidence?' I said, irritated.

Father kicked at a ball of seaweed. 'Evidence, of course, is important. If only the mystics could offer their evidence of God like the scientists do! What do you think, K?'

'Can you have evidence of such things?' said K.

'I wish I could run an experiment and find out,' said my father.

'Why don't you?' K said.

As usual, he committed nothing beyond the territory of medicine. And, there, too, he had reservations.

'You, Som, what do you think?'

'Such understanding is beyond me,' I laughed. 'Maybe, I too should run an experiment.'

I felt superior, more in control. No, totally in control, of whatever furies lurked among the savage stars or at the bottom of the sea that roared to the right of us. I had the conceit of youth because I slept ten hours, had more money than I knew of, had laid half a dozen women, because I had done all these, I felt certain I shall never get the boot. And, therefore, I was condescending. I patronized him, my father, while he struggled with the weight of the centuries. I patronized him even though I knew I hadn't the right.

'But, surely, you want to understand, Som,' my father said. It was almost a rebuke.

He had surprised me. I had always thought of him as a businessman, a chemist, perhaps brilliant, who by a fluke — Mr. Thapar had been the fluke — became a businessman. I had never imagined that he was concerned with anything other than the mystery of the molecule. What was this? This chatter about a First Cause?

Coming back after cremating him, I wandered about the empty house. I went up to his room. His spectacles lay near the night-light, the ends crossed, just as he always kept them. At the end of the room, near the wardrobe, lay the half-packed suitcase meant for his journey to Brussells, a journey that he would have undertaken at roughly that hour. From the wall his photograph with my mother, taken right after their wedding, stared down at me. He used to have short hair then. But the determined chin was there. And so, paradoxically, was the bewilderment in the eyes.

Was there a First Cause? He had wanted to know. And now? I wondered, had he found the answer by now?

5

Did Lal Haveli ever exist? Could it be a fragment of an overheated imagination, a vapour, like that little cloud beyond my window, crossing the face of the midnight moon? Were it not for the images — photographs of the soul — that pass time and again before my eyes, I might, indeed, have doubted its existence. A desolate garden; an alley; a brooding windowless facade; white-washed walls smudged with the hands of rickshaw pullers; a broken fountain, a ceiling full of unlit chandeliers; ventilators of stained glass. Where else could have I seen the sarcophagus of green marble that, even in my dreams, possesses the power to chill me? How else the idea of a labyrinth within the labyrinth of lanes that stretch westwards from the *ghats* of Benaras.

I remember being fetched from the hotel by Tarakki, Aftab's morose, reticent chauffeur. It was a warm evening. There were no avenues or landmarks or statues of statesman that I recognized. But I recognized the river and the river was always there, at every turn, disappearing momentarily from view only to reappear in a grander vista. It demanded notice — and got it. A long iron bridge, brown and red, leaned across a wilderness. Except for its black silhouette the vast evening sky was empty. On the other side of the river there were ruins and marshes, where the dacoits periodically, no doubt, plundered, also in the name of a god.

The road narrowed down. There was no kerb to mark its margins. It dribbled into dusty footpaths which, in turn, vanished into a *nullah*, a ditch, a row of shops. Shops were everywhere, little wooden structures, as high as a man. Inside them, on little cushions, sat men in black caps, their paan-red lips open like unhealed wounds. They looked up as the car went by, their eyes wide in small-town curiosity. I loathed small towns.

There were mendicants, a bewildering variety, caring neither for the car nor the other distraction of this illusory world. This was one class of humanity that Aftab's chauffeur respected even if he cared little for the laws of traffic. Mesmerized, he started at their ash-smeared bodies, drugged eyes, offering even a smart salute if they seemed inclined to receive one.

Presently, structures of brick and mortar appeared; not skyscrapers or even bungalows whose windows might shine with the reflection of the sun, but medieval facades with heavy wooden doors. They looked like the habitat of the rich. Beyond them stood little diminutive dwellings, thousands of them, perched on each other's shoulders, white and yellow and an occasional green, their sun-baked walls waiting for the night. A turn blocked out the sun and the sky, took us back three hundred years. Buildings like these did not exist in Bombay whose destiny, I knew, was addressed to different purposes.

The old Dodge twisted and turned in a maze of narrow streets. I was surprised that it could move at all. There was traffic about but it slid easily past the automobile. Before leaving, Mr. Thapar had said, 'Personally, I don't know if there is still such a lot of advantage in acquiring his company.'

'But you agree there is some advantage,' I said.

'Oh yes, of course.'

'Besides,' I added, 'I don't believe he can manage it. If it is not us, it will be someone else.'

So here I was, in an old Dodge smelling of gasoline and tobacco, rattled around by a reticent chauffeur. A fire-station, a sharp turn, and we were in a blind alley. There was a heavy antique door, its square panels studded with brass knobs. A courtyard paved with grey slate. Aftab beside a broken fountain. Dark glasses, white shirt, a striped necktie that might have belonged to a regiment of the Indian Army.

'Welcome, Bhaskar,' he said, extending his hand.

I remembered Anuradha saying, 'A Bhaskar! What is a Bhaskar doing in business?'

In the warm April evening, near the broken fountain, Aftab and I shook hands. His hand was soft and I cannot say that I did not feel a certain affection for him.

He led me inside, into a room that was cool. It was furnished in maroon. The sofas, carpets, curtains, tables, chairs, all were maroon. Anuradha sat on a maroon divan along with another woman. We exchanged smiles of recognition. She looked different from what I remembered of her: more relaxed, in control. Persian carpets lay scattered over a floor of marble. The other woman stared out of sad brown eyes. Dressed in a silk *garara*, its gold glittering in the semi-dark, she looked like a luminous extra on a film set. She stared but did not seem to take much in.

I talked of this and that, not the business that had brought me. His head thrown back Aftab smoked without a break. He listened politely. In fact, he heard nothing. Anuradha watched me. Now and then she nodded, smiled.

The Blue Room — for that was how that room of maroons was called by them — darkened, although it was still light over the fountain. The room remained unlit except for a brass lamp. A chandelier hung from the ceiling. There were other chandeliers. None of them was lit. Maroon curtains of old velvet hid the walls.

There might have been windows behind them or doors or other rooms. There were no street sounds. The room had the authority of a separate creation. This was how it might always have been: a dark brooding presence inhabited by a man, his wife, and his mistress.

While we waited for tea, I strolled towards the farther edge. There was a chess-table. A game of chess, half-way through a manoeuvre, lay upon it. A portrait of Anuradha, bright in spite of the darkness, stared down at me, the hint of a smile in her eyes. Her dress was unchanged since the days of the portrait. There were other portraits.

'What are you staring at?' Anuradha said at my back.

I turned with a start.

'You scared me. This is a fine portrait.'

'Aftab did it.'

'Oh, did he? You never know what all these plastic manufacturers do in their spare time. And who are the rest?'

'Aftab's ancestors, most of them.'

Landowners, *taluqdars,* courtiers. She led me past the silent row.

'They all seem to be the dancing-girl type,' I said.

She moved on impatiently. 'This is the portrait of Aftab's grandfather.'

'He looks exactly like him.'

'He was a great poet, a friend of... oh, what's the point? You would only think of the dancing-girls he lived with. Let's go for tea.'

Turning a corner I was startled by an apparition. Careworn, holding a cigarette in one hand, it looked as though for many centuries it had lived in that bleak house. I stared breathless, realizing, suddenly, that I was staring at my own image.

I turned around, laughed sheepishly. Anuradha had disappeared but there was Aftab.

'Come this way,' he said.

'I did not know you painted portraits.'

'Vanity of vanities. And like all vanities that, too, has passed.'

He had a nice smile but its effect, because of the goggles, was odd. It seemed as though he smiled with half a face.

We crossed a long dark corridor. Passing under a solitary bulb in the centre I turned towards him. A stray beam of light pierced his glasses and I thought I saw an eye, enormously magnified by the thick lenses. I was startled because the eye was watching me. The corridor ended in a small vine-covered patio. The vines were full of dust. Anuradha waited for us. Tea had been laid on a chipped table. We sat on black cane chairs. As I took my chair, a lizard, green and red, scurried off into the vines. Lal Haveli was an odd mixture of the decrepit and the affluent.

In the deepening dusk we took tea.

'Have you ever been inside a house like this?' Aftab said.

'No.'

'There are things about such houses that you discover only with time.'

'I am sure that's true of all houses. I haven't entered my father's room for years.'

'Your father was a very good man. A superior person.'

'Did you know him?'

'Everyone in the industry knew him.'

Anuradha spoke: 'Why can't you visit your father's room?'

'Surely, Bhaskar is not here to discuss that,' Aftab interposed.

'That's all right,' I said.

'I really want to know,' she said ignoring her husband.

'I don't know. Maybe because he died of melancholia.'

She was visibly moved. 'But why? Why that of all things?'

I shrugged.

After tea, Aftab led me into the middle of a ravaged garden. The grass was patchy and brown. Except for a monstrous peepul, it had neither trees nor shrubs nor even a bush of nettles. The peepul was very old. Long roots hung from its branches. A grinning, pink-faced, monkey hung from a branch.

'Let me take you around the haveli,' Aftab said.

The place was bigger than its narrow facade would have led one to believe. Much bigger. It must have been built over a long period. A room here. A verandah there. You could spot the idiosyncrasies of the different builders. They were eccentricities more than differences of style. A variety of balconies and cornices and patios. Doors of all shapes and colour; some carved, others painted in ornate, fading enamel. There were rooms, bright and airy as a gazebo; others where sunlight never entered. Aftab explained nothing nor did I bother to seek explanations. Noises of the city rushed in with the opening of a door; equally suddenly, they were choked off. Occasionally, I caught a passing view of a spire against the evening sky. Bits of plaster fell on us as we went past.

The house was built either with no plan or with a most meticulous plan, though directed at an elusive objective. We climbed and came down meaningless flights of stairs. Passages twisted and turned, ran through uninhabited rooms. There were terraces covered with moss, and courtyards so airless that no one could ever have sat in them. Vines had been planted in what might have been toilets at one time. There were rooms with windows of stained glass that was fashionable fifty years earlier. The rooms contained little furniture.

There was a chunk of green marble against a mottled wall. On it was carved a tall vase. Long stemmed flowers spilled out of it. The flowers were coloured with bits of glass. There was a parrot on one side of the vase and a horse on the other. At the bottom, a verse in the Arabic script was engraved. The whole piece, so like a sarcophagus, stood extraordinarily sharp amidst the dead surroundings.

We went through another set of rooms and corridors and, then, at the end of a passage, we came upon the same sarcophagus of green marble. And now the artifacts started to repeat themselves, until, I realized, that it was a maze that we were moving through. Perhaps, the entire haveli had been built as a maze. What an idea! Passing once again by the marble sarcophagus I wanted to ask Aftab what it was that the couplet said. I did not. It was as if the couplet was the seal to a mystery that would be destroyed if I were told its meaning.

And, then, as though on the rebound, I became aware of the strange, intense sensuality that, like adrenaline, the decrepit and decadent surroundings had released in my blood. Standing in an empty mezzanine with a stream of coloured lights pouring in from the ventilators, its primal intensity nearly overwhelmed me. Heaven knew what acts men and women had consummated in the seclusion of these secret chambers. In this place anything could happen. Aftab was looking at me. The spasm passed. We moved on. Coming out on some other front, we stood on a platform.

'It is all run down now, this haveli, but its labyrinth remains.'

So, it was a labyrinth.

'It certainly needs repairs,' I said.

'When we got married I brought Anuradha here. We stood on this platform. This garden was in bloom that winter. There was fruit on the trees. My father was alive and money was coming in from the lands. Things have dried up since, Anuradha stood here on this platform and cried. She could see perhaps what was coming.'

He spoke again, 'You know, Bhaskar, someone had been buying the shares of my company.'

I kept quiet.

'What should one do?'

'You should be grateful.'

He turned to look at me, fumbling for a cigarette all the while. 'You think so?' he said.

'Don't you?'

'At times I do, yes.'

I wondered if Anuradha had told him who the buyer was.

'Why don't you sell off the whole thing?'

'One might. On the other hand, one could just scrape through.'

One could also snatch the stars from heaven, I thought. 'What's the use of scraping through? You might as well have money in the bank.'

'What's the use of money in the bank?' He seemed genuinely at a loss.

'Anyway,' he added, 'Anuradha does not want me to sell.'

There was nothing to be said if they were bent upon ruining themselves. In the distance, a temple bell started to ring. Aftab said, 'And yet, you know, I might sell it off if the right man came along.'

'The only right man in business is the man with the money.'

'That's true.'

'What's your right man?'

'I don't want to discuss. I find it difficult to argue with you.'

I looked at him in surprise, a little ashamed. No one had ever said that to me.

'Why do you say that?'

'You have such strong ideas. And you hold them so... so feverishly. Why do you do that?'

He was piqued.

'I am sorry,' I said.

'Oh, that's all right.'

With that little outburst he clammed up.

We wandered leisurely back through the building. 'Did I tell you it is built like a labyrinth, this haveli.'

'You did. But why?'

'My ancestors baffled their enemies this way. There are rooms within rooms, corridors that only bring you back to where you started.'

'I noticed that. Can you really lose your way?'

'Of course. There are rooms where you could lock a man up and he would never be found. No one would hear his cry.'

'And what is in the last labyrinth?'

'In the last labyrinth?'

'Yes.'

'Why, death, of course.'

I looked at him, puzzled.

'I meant the labyrinth of this house.'

'Yes... yes...,' he said vaguely and went ahead.

We climbed up to a vast terrace. It was still light. Aftab introduced me to his city, for he was, ultimately, a child of Benaras, the Benaras of *taluqdars* and minor rajahs, as much as I was of Bombay. And Anuradha? Hers was a city without a name, a city set in an oasis, plundered a thousand times and waiting to be plundered again, by men like Aftab and me who forever lurked in its desert purlieus.

I looked around. So, this was the city that had been famous before Rome was known or Cyrus had built the Persian Empire; whose craftsmen had provided silks for King Solomon's palaces and gold for his temples? If it was so, the view from Aftab's terrace gave no hint of it. We looked smack into enormous hoardings: one advertising a movie, the other aphrodisiacs. Around them sprouted other hoardings, small and big, offering bulbs, hotels, saris, typing schools, sweet shops, hair oils, sweaters, fans, diesel engines. Surrounding the hoardings, like a fisherman's net, lay a maze of narrow lanes. The lanes were crowded, with people and with holy bulls. The houses themselves were nondescript, built in thick clusters but with a singular randomness as if they grew out of handfuls of seed that one of the city's million gods had carelessly scattered. There was a skyline, though, an impressive one. Spires, pinnacles, minarets thrust into the evening sky. *Kalashes* gleamed in the light of the sun that was setting at our backs. Scattered among these, a striking row of white buildings jutted out at all angles. They had a strange sombreness in the fading light.

'What are those buildings,' I asked Aftab.

'Widows' homes, orphanages, rehabilitation centres.'

'That is a grim list.'

He turned and looked at me in surprise. I wondered what had so surprised him.

'That is Aurangzeb's mosque. And that over there is Ganga.' He put it as though indicating a personal possession. 'They propose to build a new bridge over it.'

'That should be good.'

'One seldom knows what is good.'

Epigrams in others had always annoyed me. But Aftab put them so genuinely, so without affectation that he seemed even unaware that they were epigrams. In fact, that was the only way he talked. Did he pick them up from men like Amjad Mian? Or, from his dead ancestors, all those obsolete faces staring from the walls of the Blue Room? Or, maybe, he coined them all by himself, in the darkness of his brain. He never looked at me when he uttered them and yet, I felt, they were somehow directed at me.

'What does a bridge mean to me?' he said. 'Easier journey? But journeys to where? I dislike travel. When I was young I was expected to run about, conduct business. My father was never satisfied with what I did. I myself had the constant feeling that I was not doing enough. Maybe, I used to think, there are places I ought to see, action I should witness, decisions I should take. Now, I know better. It is a great relief to know that there is no new thing under the sun. At least, for me. For people like you it must be different.'

'I am still running around looking for some new thing under the sun.'

'I hope you find it, my friend.'

'But you do worry about shares, don't you?'

'Yes, but that is because it concerns Anuradha. She is so keen to see me succeed.'

'She wants you to be an industrialist?'

'I don't know. It is just that she can't stand to see anybody fail. It breaks her heart. So, here I am, stuck with this industry and she wants me to somehow pull through.'

A row of carts, their wooden wheels creaking, went slowly towards the *ghats.* The street directly below us must have been another alley because I hadn't seen a soul there all the while we had been sitting on the terrace. Night crept over the city. The sky here had a clarity and a panorama that I had seldom seen in Bombay. That sky and that river might have produced poets and saints, even kings, but could they have produced an industrialist? Here was a void of its own kind and Aftab's ancestors had filled it in their own way: with polished conversation and song and an occasional clash of arms. Could Aftab get away from the legacy and fill this emptiness with plastic powder?

Aftab spoke of Lucknow, of his ancient relatives draped in fine silks, riding elephants, leading the siege to the Residency. There were women and children inside but the fire that had swept Avadh did not take note of such details — on either side.

'My ancestors believed they were the true rulers of Hindustan,' commented Aftab wryly. I wondered if he, too, thought that and at times, on hot, idle evenings, looked back with rage and nostalgia at how close victory had been. Aftab's ancestors were fine soldiers, a match for the English who were camped across the river. But, unlike the English, they had no plans. They lived from day to day and impulse to impulse.

'Just like me,' said Aftab. Inside the city, dancing and drinking parties went on until one night news came that the English had made a bridgehead. The *sowars,* then, rushed out in tens and twenties and were quickly cut down. Canon balls flew through the Imambara, the palaces. Children, their backs broken by grapeshot, lay quietly down on doorsteps to die. Later, all was arson and loot. His ancestors fled — to Rohilkhand, Nepal, Benaras. Years of idleness and decadence followed. His father tried to rise from these ashes and pushed their fortunes into plastics.

Somewhere behind him this troubled and fiery past still loomed. So did the dancing girls and the music. For all I knew, he was presented with a female slave when he was fifteen.

When it was dark we came down. In the Blue Room, on the low divan, staring into the vacancy of the crepuscular darkness, sat Anuradha. Aftab went to her and put his hand on her shoulder.

'Hello,' I said.

She smiled at me, a warm friendly smile, but said nothing. Aftab sat next to her. They did not talk. Their silence had that quality of satiation that is known only to the long and happily married or among very old friends. I felt envious. Geeta was all that a wife could be and yet, somehow, I had goofed it all up.

Aftab said, 'I think I'll wash up. Make yourself a drink, Bhaskar.'

'I'll wait for you,' I told his disappearing back.

Anuradha and I stared at each other, like old adversaries, each, presumably, familiar with the other's tricks. Her direct intense gaze bristled with unspoken questions. I was the first to turn my eyes away.

That gaze had been forged for carrying out transactions of the soul. Looking at you like that she seemed to put her hand on your shoulder and invite you to open your heart, promising you all the while that there was nothing that would surprise her. She was not self-conscious about her body of whose grace and sensuousness she seemed unaware. She did not fidget about or pull at her sari like most women. A lamp burned by her side lighting up parts of her face. She looked thoughtful and tired. Coming across her like that, the idea crossed my mind that, perhaps, it was to see *her* and not to negotiate for the shares that I had really come to Benaras, and to Aftab's haveli.

I felt weary, too, after all that inspection, and a little fuzzy in the head.

'Do you like Benaras?' she said.

'Not exactly.'

'I didn't think you would come.'

'I didn't think you would invite me.'

'You have begun to talk like Aftab. Come and sit down.'

She patted the place next to her where Aftab had sat a while ago. I sat down, feeling light.

'Make yourself a drink if you like.'

'Where is Aftab?'

'He takes time getting ready for the evening.'

'This is hardly evening.'

'For the night, then. Anyway, would you like a drink?'

She pointed to a long dark cabinet. I pulled at a brass knob that stuck out of it. The cabinet door came down revealing a bar of sorts. The bottles were stacked against a mirror. For a moment, I was transfixed, staring at the reflections of our faces: one ageing and tense, the other dark-eyed, sexy, a little fatigued, like the haunting images of my childhood. She smiled into the mirror. I continued to stare at her reflection unable to break off. I knew I wanted her even if, as usual, it was just for once.

She sat up, tucked her legs under her. 'Did you manage to talk to him about the shares?' she said.

I looked at her uncertainly.

'Are you making fun of me?' I said.

'Yes.'

'I don't like that. Anyway, it was he who talked about them. He said he might have disposed of them had it not been for you. It was you who wanted him to succeed in industry, he said.'

'What is wrong with that?'

'It is what they call a misplaced enthusiasm.'

She did not catch that.

Why hadn't I talked to him about the shares which was what I had come to do? And I was to leave for Bombay the next morning. The issue had been there, alive all the time, at the back of my mind.

But it had been swamped, drowned out: by Lal Haveli, its sounds and colours, the maze of its layout and the maze of the city as I had seen it from the terrace, by the unexpected stirring in me of some long dormant essence of a different kind.

'When I was in Bombay last month I ran into Geeta,' she said.

'You did!'

'At K's clinic. She said you were standing for the presidentship of the Association.'

'Should I?'

'How should I know?' she laughed.

'Don't laugh,' I said. 'I really want to know.'

'You should. You are made for such things. Maybe, that is all that you want.'

She leaned sideways reaching for a box. It was made of silver and looked like a *paandan*. She opened it and took out a cigarette. As I bent forward to light it for her I noticed how well her *choli* fitted her. A very fine gold chain glowed around her throat and on her chest and disappeared between the full breasts. If she was aware of my gaze she took no notice of it.

'That is a curious looking box,' I said.

She handed it to me. 'Aftab's father gave it to us. It is a hundred years old.'

'It certainly looks it.'

It was heavy, mysterious, made of solid silver. It shone with a dull glow. Its lid was brazed with round silver coins, the kind I had seen in the museums of the Nizam. There were things written in Persian on the coins and on the sides of the box. I resisted the temptation of asking her what it was that was written on the box. I opened the lid.

'And these are curious looking cigarettes.'

Anuradha smiled, and, to my surprise, blushed.

'They look delicious,' I said.

She nodded slowly, letting out smoke.

'I just visited the spot where you cried the day you were married,' I said.

'Married?' she laughed. 'I have never been married.'

For a moment I was too confused to speak.

'Aren't you and Aftab married?'

'Of course not. I just live with him.'

'I see.'

She was a nice attractive person and there was a vitality in her that had drawn me so. It seemed a pity that she should be nobody's wife.

'It is better not to be anybody's wife,' she said as if reading my thoughts. She had a way, I discovered later, of commenting on things that you had yet to put into words. 'You can't marry everyone you love. So, why marry anyone at all?'

That sounded like Leela Sabnis.

'But if you have never been married why should Aftab mention it?'

'One of Aftab's little make-beliefs. That's all. You have your own.'

'What?'

'Make-beliefs.'

'Yes,' I said. 'Yes.' I rose to make another drink.

There was the sound of a harmonium somewhere in the haveli. A woman's voice rose and fell. I stood against the little bar and again looked at Anuradha. The muted light of the lamp fell across her, throwing her shadow on the velvet cushions and on the wall. With her old jewellery and antique clothes she looked like a ghost from long ago. She was smoking, thinking. The light in the room had not changed. The shadows clung to their appointed places. So did the furniture. Anuradha looked up, 'You are watching me again.'

'Yes. You are very good looking.'

'Oh!'

'Tell me something. Why is this house made like this?'

'Made like what?'

'In this hotch-potch way.'

She was puzzled.

'I don't understand. I have not noticed anything unusual. It is an old haveli.'

'It is made like a labyrinth, Aftab says.'

'That is another of his make-beliefs. He likes the idea of a *bhul-bhulaiyan.* Once we visited the Bhul-bhulaiyan of Lucknow. We wandered a long time through it, over and over, one whole afternoon. It was evening when we came out. Aftab was exhausted but he was excited as he never gets excited. When we came back, he said, "Isn't this built like a *bhul-bhulaiyan,* too?" Now he shows people round this haveli as though it were a labyrinth.'

'The strange thing is, it seemed like a labyrinth to me, too.'

'Maybe, the two of you have something in common,' she smiled, playing with the chain around her neck.

'Aftab even has a view on what is in the last labyrinth.'

'What is that?'

'Death, he says.'

'Oh! The two of you really have something in common.'

Aftab entered through an unlit entrance. He greeted me, putting his hand on my shoulder.

'We have met before, you know,' I said, taking his hand in mine.

'I know. It is such a pleasure meeting you. Every time it seems like the first time. Would you like to go to the *ghats* now?'

'Now?'

'Yes.'

It was late but Aftab was a creature of the night.

~

At twenty two I had patronized my father. Ten years later, at the hour nearing midnight, the sight of all those funeral pyres on the Manikarnika Ghat, the smell of burning flesh and bursting of bones, gave me one big shaking down before I got hold of myself. The flames, lighting this, hiding that, throwing crazy shadows all over, made matters worse. And in that shaking down, I sort of went stiff and, going down a step, keeled a little, knocking my arm against Anuradha's bangles. For a passing second, I thought she curled her fingers around my wrist, as though steadying me. I turned but she was looking straight ahead where Aftab threaded down the steep steps, leading the way. Anuradha was relaxed, lost in heaven knew what happy thoughts. What filled me was the dread, cold sweat and a familiar turbulence.

I had my reasons for the cold sweat as well as the turbulence. Some months earlier, as the doctors put it, I had had my 'little incident.'

I had woken up one night choking, scared to death. When I climbed steps I had pain in the chest. Finally, K took cardiograms. They were all right to start off. Then they started to go haywire. Within the hour I was in the hospital, plugged with a dozen shots. Geeta was there, distraught, holding back the tears, probably praying. Here goes another, she must have thought. Some years earlier her brother had been killed. I had never loved her more.

I was a month in the nursing home and it was a nasty month, the worst yet. The drugs got me; there was no end to them. The first thing in the morning was a shot. The last thing at night was a shot. They depressed the hell out of me, those drugs. I felt weepy all the time. When the drugs eased the staff took over. The nurses were a rum lot, one stiffer-arsed than the next. Yet, you couldn't do without them. All you wanted to do was to get away. And, that was precisely what you could not do. So, you kept wondering about what was happening to you. For instance, why this little 'incident'? True, my father had a bad heart but why had I been touched so *early?* By what right? What was now to happen to my pursuit of fame? Had I been once and for all shoved off the stage, away from the footlights, packed off to some dark dusty corner in the wings; or some dingy green room where I was to put on a new make up, several cuts below that of a prince that I had set out to be. At the same time, though, I felt a new loathing for the squalid world that carried on beneath my hospital window. All those buses and cars and taxis and men scurrying back and forth like cockroaches. For what? But if it was loathing, then why that longing to get right back among the vermin as soon as possible? More than anyone else, it was K and Geeta who pulled me through. At the end of it all, I had begun to wonder if I at all deserved such a fine woman.

The voids during that illness had never loomed larger. Not just without. Also within.

It is the voids of the world, more than its objects, that bother me. The voids and the empty spaces, within and without. First, it was only the voids without: empty mountain sides, stretches of oceans, beaches, unsown fields, alleys after dark, corridors of hospitals, the hum against the ear of a conch, caves. That was how it had probably started — with the caves. I was home that summer. I was eighteen. I was alone in a cave at Ajanta. It wasn't one of the showpieces. I must have gone in for a break from the sun. It was cool inside and dark. Then the walls started to float in, trembling, shimmering, daubed here and there with colour. The colours were faint, as they are in dreams. I had stood there trying to make sense out of them. And then, as gradually as they had materialized, the walls dissolved into the darkness. I continued to stand there until I was cooler. The walls came and went in dizzy waves, the daubs of colour dancing before my eyes. The spasms of darkness grew steadily longer. Or, so it had seemed. Finally, I could not stand it any longer. When the wall disappeared once again I dashed out.

Voids of caves and voids of the sky; the terrible vacancies of *lokalok*. That same summer, on my way back to America I flew from Tokyo to Honolulu. It had been nine p.m. in Tokyo. Three hours later, over the quiet waters of the Pacific, a dawn met us. It was an ordinary dawn, gentle, even picturesque, but something in its coming, so totally without notice, disturbed me. It lit up the empty spaces of the sky like a candle does the dome of a tomb. It lit up those empty spaces so I have never forgotten them.

And here, on Manikarnika, were voids with a bang. Both within and without. That was probably how it had always been except that I had been too cocky to notice. You have to have a little 'incident' or get a telephone at midnight about so and so popping off or catch your wife with another man or be told you have cancer to see the voids within. It was the voids and not the guava groves that I had walked through that morning my mother died; and voids too in her room in Bombay; and voids each time an affair ended; and the morning my daughter was born, and on and on. Voids all.

We had gradually been moving up the steps, away from the burning corpses. The *ghats* were not deserted as I had imagined. There were men about. And animals. Even an occasional woman, wrapped from head to foot in the shroud of her sari. The men, in counterpoint, wore little. Oblivious of their surroundings, lost in the oddest of activities, they would have been taken for the inmates of a nut-house in any other country. Across the steps, in a staggered row, half a dozen men, their marvellous oiled bodies faintly gleaming, barrelled through a marathon of calisthenics. A young Sanskrit scholar recited hymns at the top of his voice. I thought of my father and his little book of the *Upanishads*. Another boy, equally young, corrected him. Did Panini ever live in Benaras? Behind the scholars, two young men, drowned in *bhang*, did a fancy jig. Boatmen, jugglers, vagrants, monkey men, idlers, beggars, flutists, bathers, the watchers of funeral pyres, junkies, medicine men, vendors, each sat in his appointed place, as if on a stage, performing parts that they had performed over the millennia. What chance did I have here of making Aftab change his mind about the shares?

We had been going up and down the steps without my being able to grasp Aftab's purpose. Very likely, he had done, just as he had done during that visit to the dargah. There was a temple where *aarati* was being performed. Outside, on the granite threshold, looking like a mauve ghost, a woman wailed and beat her shaved head against the wall. As we passed I thought she was going to touch me.

'For God's sake,' I cried in annoyance.

'Ah, Bhaskar,' said Aftab in mild rebuke. 'What do you know of sorrow?'

'What does this have to do with sorrow?' I snapped.

He kept quiet.

Beyond the temple, we again went down a series of granite steps at the bottom of which I suddenly found myself in the hollow of a boat. Aftab and Anuradha sat on the middle plank. I sat facing them. Without a word the *mallah*, a shadowy naked figure with oars in the far corner, pulled out. Anuradha, head covered, sat perfectly still. She hadn't said a word since we came to the *ghats*.

A little distance away from the bank, and it was all very quiet. It was as though we had passed through an acoustical screen. The reflections of the *ghat* lights were also left behind. I could not see the boatman's face but I could see the movement of his powerful arms. The boat left no wake behind. The eerie *chhup chhup* of the oars was the only sound. I felt as though I had moved not two hundred yards, but two hundred miles from the town of Benaras, from all towns, from the planet itself. I felt as though this was not Ganga but some unknown stream, in some unknown segment of the universe, leading to a reality that I had not yet known.

At midstream the *mallah* paused. He probably needed rest. I wondered which way we were heading: downstream or across the river. When we started again I knew we were going across. A light had appeared on the other bank. It grew bigger as we approached. It was for this light, I realized, and not to rest, that the *mallah* had paused.

The boat slid gently into the reeds of a backwater. A young girl stood on the shore waving a lantern. The *mallah,* a dark powerful man, jumped ashore, tied the boat to a stake. One after the other, he helped us get off. The girl greeted us. She wore a sari although she seemed too young for it.

'Why aren't there *ghats* on this bank of the river?' I asked as we followed the girl.

‘This bank isn’t sacred,’ Aftab replied briefly.

I had the impression no one wanted to talk. A hundred yards inland, we came upon an enclosure with a wooden gate. It looked like an orchard of sorts. There was an old peepul tree, like the one in Aftab’s back garden. In the shadow of the peepul stood a simple white-washed grave. The moonlight fell directly on it. I had already seen too many dead bodies to be shocked. A cottage had been built beyond the peepul. Into this, led by the young girl, we now went.

A large room made up most of the cottage. It was pleasantly bright with the light of a petromax. At one end of the room sat a fair, rosy woman of about forty, reading an enormous book. She was dressed in white. She looked up as we came in, acknowledging the deferential greetings with a charming smile. I did not think I had seen such a warm and generous smile for a long long time. Anuradha went nearer and touched her feet.

They did not introduce me to her. In fact, there was very little conversation. Anuradha and the young girl were the only ones to talk. They discussed a recent fair that the girl had been to. Aftab did not smoke but neither did he talk. The woman went back to her reading. Half an hour later, it seemed it was suddenly time to go. Everyone stood up as though they had heard a bell. There were the same respectful good byes and the same marvellous smile. The woman looked at me a long time as one might look at an old acquaintance.

6

The shares, what is happening to the shares? Mr. Thapar is not moving fast enough. Of course, he does not understand why, after a gap of six months, I have asked him to start buying again. ‘The prices are ridiculously high,’ he told me on telephone. ‘Why did you stop buying when they were reasonable?’ Why indeed? Why did I get humbugged? By Anuradha? By Aftab? By that woman,

Gargi whom I had visited that night on the other bank of Ganga six months ago? Maybe, I am unfair to Gargi. She probably had nothing to do with all that happened. And, yet, it was in that cottage of hers that night, that I had first felt my will beginning to weaken, the will to capture Aftab's company. Back at the haveli, squatting beside a hand pump, washing my face, the thought had crossed my mind for the first time: Is it worth the bother?

Anuradha, holding her sari between the knees, laughed and pumped the ancient hand pump. The cold water soaked through my hair, ran down my face, dripped into the collar of my shirt. Anuradha handed me a towel. She watched me as I dried myself. From the direction of the Blue Room came the sound of a sarangi being tuned.

'So we are going to have a concert now, are we?' I said.

'Aftab likes to entertain his guests.'

'I hope I shall get a few minutes after the concert to talk to him about those shares,' I said half-heartedly.

Anuradha smiled. 'I can get you a kurta of Aftab's if you want.'

'Not just now.'

Anuradha introduced me to Azizun and her niece, a girl of thirteen or fourteen. (Were they, too, a part of the conspiracy?) I had met Azizun on arrival but I had yet to hear her speak. She smiled at everybody and salaamed me, which took me by surprise. It was a moment before I could reply with a clumsy wave of the hand. She was dressed in the same *garara.* She sat on a carpet, her legs to one side, straight-backed, silent. Once again, in that dark room, I was struck by the singular phosphorescence of her face, her teeth, her dress. For all the precision of her art she had a vagueness about her that spoke of a child's mind that had been stunted by the despair of the grown-ups, even though the body matured and learnt to participate in the pleasures of the world. 'Anuradha is my brains; Azizun, ah! Azizun is the song,' declared Aftab suddenly, as though adding to Azizun's introduction. He and Anuradha now slid down from the divan. They sat facing me, all three of them, looking at me, weighing me. Azizun had coarse features. Her fair skin seemed more bloodless than ever. Aftab had brought with him a scent of flowers. He was dressed in a silk kurta and *churidars*. But those simple clothes created an effect of opulence that I did not understand. In the darkness of the room he had an imposing presence. He might indeed have been a prince. On his little toe, incredibly, he wore a diamond ring. And now that I was seeing him for the first time without his western clothes, I realized how small, soft and delicate, he actually was. In a slow, graceful movement he leaned forward and put his hand on my shoulder. 'He is handsome, isn't he?' he said to Anuradha, as though admiring a child. Anuradha looked at me, her black eyes sparkling. It seemed as though she, too, had asked a question and waited for the reply. In fact, they had the air not so much of hosts as of inquisitors. What was I to make of them, a dumb-looking singing girl, a goggled ex-nawab? I felt silly and isolated. 'Well?' I said, looking at each face in turn.

They seemed not to hear me. Nor did they talk among themselves. 'You live in a disaster area of life,' old Leela Sabnis used to say. To me my habitat had always seemed natural. Sitting there, though, watching the trio against the maroon draperies I thought maybe here were lives free of disaster, unless it came in the guise of a businessman grabbing their company. I felt bad I had not been able to find a more painless point of contact with them.

Anuradha offered the silver cigarette-box to Aftab and, then, to me. I picked one of those 'delicious' hand-rolled cigarettes.

Was this maroon Blue Room a part of the labyrinth, too? If so, what was I doing here amidst these strangers? If someone, man or god, had watched my life from a great height, would I have appeared to him like an ant threading through a maze, knocking about, against one wall, then another? Were there spirits buried in these walls, deep down in forlorn dungeons? My mother believed in spirits. So probably did these people. If only one knew! If only miracles were to take place, as of old, and one could suddenly, irrefutably, know. Without nagging, enervating doubts. I want. I want. If only one knew what one wanted. Or, maybe, to *know* was what I wanted. To know. Just that. No more. No less. This, then, was a labyrinth, too, this going forward and backward and sideways of the mind. I felt again the faint stirrings of a curiosity that I had first felt near the marble sarcophagus, a secret curiosity that I dare not share with another.

And who were these people — friendly yet remote — radiating an aura that was sensual at one moment and faintly menacing the next and something else altogether the next? Behind them, in the long tunnel of darkness, a flicker of light, like the sparks of a firefly, flashed occasionally. Gradually, the sparks increased, changed colour. From gold to red and green and violet. The flickers combined to form shapes, then uncoupled and formed other shapes. The shapes, too, coupled and uncoupled until the whole space was filled with dancing, writhing sparks. Some remote part of me had come alive. Those were excellent cigarettes.

Sometime later — I don't know how much later — Azizun was singing. Each word, each phrase, came through distinctly, like freshly poured type. I could see each word being moulded by her lips. I watched its flight as it travelled a little distance and fell in its destined place, there among the Persian carpets.

They were sad songs, all of them, sung with great sorrow, until one felt that life itself was somehow fatalistically tied down by them, that life offered no possibilities aside from those delineated by these songs, that all struggle was futile. Floating about the dark air, they carried with them their particular dementia, their frightening power to push men into despair, from despair to decadence and, thence, into madness and death. I knew I had heard those songs before.

Old Leela, too, was crazy for music. She had a great collection of records. Music always turned her on: Rock, and hard rock, and soul and, of course, the Beatles. 'The drums, the guitars, the voices,' she used to say, 'set some bit or the other of me vibrating, just as the tantrik rituals do.'

'What do the tantrik rituals do?' I had asked. Leela was a scholar and she explained but she did not much care for them. Descartes and tantras did not mix.

Azizun sang on, unaware to all appearances, of the beauty of the songs or of her own voice. It was husky, a little nasal, and it reminded you of that core of loneliness around which all of us are built. It might have emerged from the slums of Benaras but centuries had gone into its perfection. It rode the night like a searchlight, lighting up the ruins of an ancient abandoned city with which I, too, was familiar. All my life, at intervals, I, too, had flown across its blacked out skies, flapping my weary wings, not able, for all the striving, to chart a course. This city, at least, we had in common, Azizun and I. And, through Azizun, I shared it with the other two, who sat at once intent and lost, in a cloud of cigarette smoke. I could see, with sudden and unparalleled lucidity, that our difference apart, shares or no shares, we belonged to the same benighted underside of the world.

It were Azizun's songs, therefore, that made me drop my guard — for where was the question of guards among fellow creatures of the night — so that, later, when Aftab said to me, 'Bhaskar, stay with us, don't go back to the hotel,' I agreed. They had me, I suppose, where they had wanted me all along.

Still later, the girl was dancing, a mere child, thin and wispy in her costume of kathak dancer. Her little feet, so like a pair of pink birds, played with the smooth floor. The *ghunghrus* mingled with the wail of the sarangi, kept beat with the tablas. Her eyes, the neck, the full mouth and the little hands, gesticulated, suggested, built up, gesture by gesture, beat by beat, a little sensuous fire. It was stoked, this handful of embers by the music and Azizun, and by the girl herself and the long hand-rolled cigarettes. Gradually, it was stoked into a raging fire. The fire raged even when the music and the dance came to a crashing end. There was applause. The girl went to Aftab who kissed her hair and her throat and held her tiny waist in his two hands, as one might hold a lover's. Then, they were gone, Aftab and the child. A little later, Azizun went away with the musicians. Besides the ornate lamp, the silver box between us, Anuradha and I stared at each other.

'I am stoned,' I said.

She smiled, then, laughed. 'So am I,' said she.

I kissed her hand, her arm, breathing in great gulps, her strange perfume.

She smiled. The solitaire glittered in the dim light. She took my face in her hands, looked down at me from the divan.

'Yes, very handsome,' she said as though she appraised a photograph.

'Where do you get this fancy perfume?' I asked her.

'From Lucknow. Why?'

'It is marvellous but terribly sad-making.'

'You are a sad man.'

'Nobody has ever called me sad,' I laughed.

She continued to look at me in silence, then, 'Why do you want to get mixed up with riff-raff like us?' she said.

'I like you very much.'

'You don't have to say that.'

'I mean it.'

'Let me show you to your room,' she said, standing up, letting go of me.

~

I sat on a bed, in a room bright with coloured lights. The light came from behind the stained glass panes of the ventilators. The intensity of light rose and fell. The room had a cement floor of dark red and smudgy walls. An old ceiling fan turned slowly creaking every time at the same point.

'It is not very comfortable,' Anuradha said. She got ready to leave and I panicked.

'Don't go away,' I cried. 'Not just now.'

'I have to go. It is late.'

'Sit down. I'll tell you a story.'

She hesitated, then sat down on the edge of the bed. It struck me that, maybe, she wasn't in a hurry to go anywhere, that she was neither sleepy nor was there anyone waiting for her.

'Well, what is the story?'

'You know, I met you twenty years ago. In a little house by a forest. Twenty years ago.'

I fell silent.

'Is that all? Is that the story?'

I told her of the headmaster's wife and the *mehndi* on her hands.

'That was the first thing I noticed about you.'

'That is not very flattering!'

'We all have our hang-ups. Do you still have *mehndi* on your palms?'

I took her hands. There was no trace of *mehndi* there.

'Where is she now? Your headmaster's wife.'

'They migrated to Canada. I never saw her again.'

'K says your mother died of cancer.'

'Cancer and Krishna.'

'Krishna?'

'The God. My mother believed Krishna would cure her and flushed her capsules down the toilet. Krishna sat on top of her bureau and smiled and smiled, and smiled until she was dead.'

The coloured panes flared up again.

'Why do the lights behind those ventilators go up and down?'

'There is a house there that the owner rents out for marriages.'

The flare was followed by a new darkness.

'Do you believe in miracles?' I asked her.

'I don't know.'

'You believe in God?'

'I used to think of Krishna a lot.'

'So did my mother. So does Geeta.'

'Most women do.'

'But Krishna never comes,' I couldn't help mocking.

'That is true,' said Anuradha absently. 'Krishna never comes.'

There was a silence, as though Krishna was what we had met to discuss. Once again, I was afraid she would leave. I wanted to hold her as long as possible.

'Where are you from?'

'Hasn't Mr. Thapar told you?'

'He did not know.'

'He will find out some day. He is like a weasel, always digging up people's pasts. I am more scared of him than I am of you.'

I was greatly moved by what she had said.

'Don't be scared of me. Please.'

I tried to kiss her but she moved away, annoyed.

Beside the bed lay a fine carpet which I just seemed to notice. Its colours, enriched in the coloured glow, floated up against the red floor. A peacock, its tail unfurled, stood woven into it. I could see his beige claws and pink eyes and circles of emerald and ruby and cobalt on its plume. On his belly lay the copper ash-tray into which we had been dropping our cigarette butts. To the little heap Anuradha now added another and turned to me. It might have been a trick of the lighting but she looked much older, older than me and Aftab, not so much physically as by her demeanour, by the look in her eyes. It was as though she had been gifted with a special vision, a vantage point high above the earth, from where she could see the melee below as ordinary men could not. And it was as though the vision always left her sadder, taking away from her the hope and the laughter with which she had been born. I knew I wanted her.

'It is not me you want,' she said quietly, startling me with the suddenness of her remark.

'How do you know?'

'I know. You want something. You badly want something. I could see that the first time we met. But it is not me. That, too, I can see. I told you so in the dargah.'

It was my turn to be annoyed.

'O.K.,' I said. 'O.K. Forget it. You aren't going to make a difference anyway.'

'Don't be angry,' she said.

She looked distressed, in a way, guilty.

I jumped off the bed feeling a new lightness of body and mind. I walked to the window in my socks and flung it open. The cool air refreshed me. The room was at the very edge of the haveli. To the left of me, twenty feet away, ran a boundary wall of mossy old bricks. On the other side stood the house, which was rented to wedding parties. It was a single storeyed structure with a large verandah in the front. The verandah was deserted except for an old man and odd bits of furniture that lay scattered about, like sets on a stage. In one corner of the verandah, on an iron pole, hung a fierce gaslight. There were similar poles in the other three corners. They probably hung gaslights on the other poles as well whenever a wedding took place. To the right of me lay the large decrepit garden, the ghostly peepul in its centre.

I breathed deeply, taking in the fresh, cool air. I was disgusted with them, with myself, with those dissolute cigarettes whose perfume clung to my fingers. I was disgusted with letting myself be touched by their decadence. I felt dirty and bitter. I knew I should have gone back to the hotel. I was, of course, obsessed with her, just as I had been obsessed with all those other women. The one-shot obsession. It had been different with Geeta but that too had not exactly been a resounding success. I would be glad when morning came and I was off.

At that hour, the grounds of Aftab's haveli looked like the wilderness that surrounds abandoned tombs. The peepul reminded me of that other peepul across the river. I heard her move behind me, the silk of her sari rustling against her thighs. I did not turn when she came and stood by mv side.

'Tell me,' I said, 'who was that woman we went to meet across the river?'

'You mean Gargi?'

'Who is she? I thought I had met her somewhere.'

'You could not have!'

'Who is she, anyway?'

'Her father was a sufi, a pir. He lived with Aftab's father. He gave Aftab whatever sight he has.'

'He was blind, was he?'

'More or less.'

'Where did he come from?' Once again, against my will, I was drawn helplessly into the labyrinth of their mysterious world.

'The pir?'

'Yes.'

'I don't know, I never met him. Before he became a pir, they say, he was the prince of a small state. He ran away from home, took to drink. Even now you meet people who say they saw him drunk in the streets of Benaras. "When I am drunk," he would say, "when I am drunk Allah comes to me, stares at me but says nothing. So I drink the more. One day He will speak to me." '

Anuradha fell silent. We stared at the moon-washed garden.

'Then?'

'He fell ill, burnt with drink. "God does not exist," he now told people. "If he exists let Him give me a sign." His father sat by him day and night. One evening, the ceremony of the final parting was conducted between the father and the son. That night, it is said, the father had a dream. A dervish told him to give up what he loved most and God will restore his son. In the morning, the father called the mullah and his wife and he went around his son's bed three times and prayed to God that his life may please be taken and his son's spared. The next day he fell ill. His son gradually recovered. On his deathbed the father called his son and told him, "You had asked for a sign. God has given it to you." The son got well, disappeared for a few years. When he returned Aftab's father persuaded him to live with him.'

I stared out of the window. It was very quiet. 'That sounds like Babar and Humayun.'

She said nothing. My voice had sounded much too loud to my ears and I lowered it to a whisper.

'Was that his grave near the cottage?'

'Yes.'

'You believe this... this story?'

'I don't know. Probably.'

'You really do!' I laughed.

'I don't know,' she said wearily. 'You don't realize that I don't understand the way you talk. I cannot argue with you. I will never be able to argue with you. I don't even know the words that can argue with you. But you go on and on.'

I was surprised at her outburst. Something had upset her.

'I go on and on about what?'

'I don't know about what. But let me tell you something: You are not as clever as you think. You are wrong about many things. You are wrong even about yourself. You think you know a lot, when, in fact, you don't.'

After a pause she said, 'Why don't you leave us alone?'

'I am leaving tomorrow — and *not* coming back.'

'You mean you are not interested in Aftab's business?' She was all attention.

'Mr. Thapar can handle Aftab's business.'

'What did you come here for?'

'I came because of you, I think.'

'Me?'

'Yes, I wanted to meet you again, I now realize.'

I had no face to save now. I would be gone in another few hours and I would never see her again.

'I did not know that,' she said slowly.

'You know now.'

She stepped forward. I touched the bangles on her wrist, I counted them, one after the other, as one might count on the abacus. From her bangles I looked up into her large wondering eyes.

'Stay with me,' I said trying to keep the note of desperation out of my voice.

'No. No,' she said, her voice suddenly rude. She pushed me away, and was gone.

7

There are the wanters of this world and there are the givers. And, often, the wanters, I know, don't recognize the givers, or the givers the wanters. And, most times, the wanters don't even know that they are wanters or the givers that they are givers. And if they know, they are too shy to admit. Or, too proud. And so they wander the streets of the world, on opposite pavements, burnt in their hunger, to take or to give, and do not lift their gaze and, finally, fall in the dust of the road. So it goes.

Frustrated, standing at the window, watching the old man in the 'house of weddings' I thought of Geeta. She would have enjoyed the Pir story. Of late, she had become a great enthusiast of temples, shrines, tombs of the godly. Ten years with me and she had developed her own guide-book of grief. Saints, sadhus, miracle-workers, astrologers, they drew her. Was it my rages that had driven her? My fornications? Her brother's death? Or some urges of her own? Where she had every right to the adulteries of the body she had only taken to the cleansing of the soul.

Geeta, of course, is a great, big giver herself. As big as they come. Between Anuradha and her it must have been love at first sight. If discontent is my trademark, trust is Geeta's. She is an intelligent person, sophisticated, aware of the pitfalls of the world. Why then this trust in the world's mechanisms, this faith that the engine shall not seize, or worse, explode?

Geeta trusts like birds fly, like fish swim.

It was this trust of hers — in me, in life — that had drawn me. Beside the swimming pool of the Cricket Club, to be precise. It enveloped her, this trust, like the amniotic fluid envelopes the embryo, protecting her slim shanks and tender white arms. It was stamped on her swimming suit, so modest amidst the grossness that lay about. It exuded from her small breasts — so different from Anuradha's — and if she had removed her dark glasses I would have found it radiating from her two eyes, like the beams of a lighthouse.

If trust could navigate men through the storms of the spirit, I would have weathered them all.

But I needed the trust — who doesn't? I needed it all the more because I did not trust myself, or my men, or my fate, or the ceaseless travel on the social wheel. Between the empty home and the cluttered offices — so many men, unknown, unknowable, each with a quiver of axes to grind — between these two poles of existence, friendless in a city that I did not love and which, for that matter, did not love me, even though it eyed my money, in this whore of a city what I needed most was to be reassured that all was well.

It was September. Sultry and warm. I went to a fair; no, a fete, a fete for the dead of a war, laid out in a lawn full of stones and yellow grass. There were stalls, the kind that clutter the fetes for the dead. Handicrafts. Brasswork. Children's clothes. *Chaat.* Hand-printed saris. A stall for contests whose rules no one understood and hence whose prizes nobody won. Through the stalls, threading each with the next, rushed old Parsi ladies. There were young girls, too, bright young things. I wandered about, losing patience by the minute, looking for one Mrs. Bedi, for whom I had brought a cheque. Why couldn't they make her stand in the front? Twenty five thousand rupees was no chicken-feed. I gave her two minutes to show up. Two minutes or I would go. I had better things to do.

There was a stall of silent, vacant-eyed dolls. Beyond it lay an enclosure, bounded on three sides with red *shamianas*. There, in neat rows, in a vacancy that seemed an extension of the vacancy of the doll's shop, sat a hundred women, shrouded in white, and in a silence that rang louder than the tumult around.

Astonished, I stared at the women and they at me. Then one came forward.

I said I was looking for Mrs. Bedi.

'I am Mrs. Bedi,' she said.

She was plump, grey-haired, rosy-cheeked, a bit like Gargi. I fumbled in my pockets forgetting which contained the cheque.

'This is our contribution,' I said, shaken by those terrible rows of muslin. Mrs. Bedi did not look at the cheque but folded her hands.

'Thank you. It will be of great help to all of us.'

I turned to go, then turned back, confused and upset. 'Listen,' I said, trying not to show my nerves. 'This isn't much. We shall do more. Raise more money, I mean. Soon. Tell me where I can get in touch with you.'

'It is kind of you,' Mrs. Bedi said. She gave me the address.

Stepping out of the enclosure, hurrying, aware at my back of the gaze of the hundred whom death had undone, I began to dump my armour, the shields and the swords, the coats of mail. By the time I passed the stall of the dolls again, I was stripped naked. In the stall, trembling, I came upon Geeta, holding a brown teddy bear, a badge on her shoulder, alive and smiling, surrounded by a multitude of glass eyes. We looked at each other. Around us the fete swirled, mounting every few minutes a notch or two, towards some final climax when, through the *rangoli*-strewn gates, a Minister would come and, ensconced between chiffoned women, would address the widows' silence.

'Come, let us go,' I said.

'Go where?' Geeta said, taken aback.

'Anywhere. To your house. To the movies. Anywhere.'

We went to her house and had dinner with her parents. Her father made small talk. Her mother was shy but alert. She tried more than her husband, to make me feel at home. Their son, she said, was at the front.

After dinner I took Geeta out. I did not know where I was taking her. It was not very late. The city was still awake, not that it ever slept, tying up the day's transactions, unlocking the coffers of the night, putting out such charms as it possessed, stirring its octopus arms, in pursuit of little pleasures or little vendettas, or even that aimless wandering that filled the hearts of its youth — the clerks, the shop girls, the unemployed. They milled about the shop fronts and board-walks, eager for life. Through all this we cruised, Geeta and I, in the Mercedez that had been my father's, Geeta sitting as far away from me as the seat would allow. I avoided the horn: that was the least that I could do for them, the wanderers. And at one point I said to Geeta: 'How do you think it feels to be young and spend the finest evenings of one's life beating the pavements, hungering and empty-handed?'

'I don't know,' she replied.

No, Geeta is no waffler. Not by a long shot. No bogus shaman to the sorrows of men, no candidate for the thrones of judgement that I have been only too eager to jump into.

We didn't say much as we drove. Geeta did not know where we were going. Nor, for that matter, did I. Through the neon-lit streets, narrow and wide, I coursed, drifting north. Near Mahim, while I waited before a traffic light, the sweet stench of the slaughter houses wafting through the car, I thought of the Maya.

It had been bought for the peace and the quiet of my mother. It was here that she spent her last days. Here, one afternoon, when she was young and not ill, she came out from the bath in a robe and sat before the mirror while I brushed her hair. She kissed me on the ear and called me a beautiful boy. When she died my father put a telescope on the roof and, to kill his insomnia, started to track the stars.

The lawns of the Maya were unkempt. I did not have my father's interest in lawns. Geeta stumbled on a sun-dial, another of his toys. We stepped on to the verandah and sat down. The chowkidar stared at Geeta, appraising her. Geeta ran no danger. The old man recognized her, knew her class. Doors were unlatched, windows flung open, all lights switched until the cottage glowed like a liner at anchor. We sat in the verandah.

'He looked suspicious,' Geeta said indicating the chowkidar.

'I had brought a woman here once,' I explained. 'A woman off the streets.'

We stared at each other. I realized that I was waiting. I was waiting for the reaction. And in that instant it burst upon me that she meant more to me than I had imagined. I was not one to care for people's reactions unless they meant something to me.

In her lap, Geeta shifted her hands. I continued to wait. But that was all. No reproach or alarm or blase nonchalance. Only a shift of the hands and that enduring trust, sending out its unfailing lasers.

Is there a theory of mate-selection — not the Freudian stuff that old Leela was so keen on — something simpler, nearer to the plays of fate? Why does one man look into a girl's eyes, another at her horoscope, a third at her father? For me that shift in the clasp of the hands was enough. If not enough, a long way to enough. Here was no ordinary girl. I thought I needed to explain. 'It was a mistake,' I said, 'I was drunk and unhappy.'

She said nothing.

A little later we went into the cottage.

Sofas, chairs, tables, lamps, paintings, books, curtains fluttering in the breeze, my mother's sarod, photographs, magazines, cupboards whose contents I had yet to examine, mirrors, radios, carpets, ash trays, (one of them filled with stubs), a rose-wood cabinet that, I knew, contained an astronomer's camera, a collection of the world's coins, sculpture, a bit of antique jewellery, the kind that Anuradha wore, my grandfather's gun.

You walk into your parent's house after they are dead and the house starts talking. As we passed, visitors to this carnival of fossils, this other fete for the dead, I felt my senses sharpening. There was a steel cupboard that I had come rummaging one gloomy evening, looking for the deed of K's trust. It lay on the middle shelf on top of the leather-bound minute-book that I am now writing in. Maybe it is not a minute-book but a diary. Why should my father keep a totally blank minute-book in that cupboard of maximum security. 'K suggests I should keep a daily diary,' he told me once. 'Whatever for?' I had said. Maybe he wanted to record his experiment about the First Cause. In any case, it is a fine piece of stationery, as good as they come.

At the end of a corridor, on a pedestal in a corner, stood Krishna, carved in wood, ankles crossed, playing an imaginary flute.

All my life I have heard voices. I don't mean I am loony. I hear them just like everyone else except that, maybe, I hear them a little too often and a little too loud. Voices, mostly of the dead. That is another thing I don't like about them but in this sort of business you can't pick and choose. So I hear the voices of dead people: relatives, authors, scoundrels, saints, of people who had never existed — characters out of novels, gods, demons. I let them chatter, carry on their brain-washing. But at times they get under my skin. I put up a resistance then. Shut up, I tell them. Shut up. Shut up. Shut up. If they don't, I try and muzzle them or jam them like countries jam each other's broadcasts: or I get drunk and get away from them. And there, in that narrow room, in the crepuscular darkness, beyond the sculpture of Krishna, were whispers, such a thick barrage, that I was suddenly fighting back with all my strength.

That was where my mother had lived for six months, refusing to go to a hospital. She communed with astrologers while the cancer ate away her lungs. There was quacks, too, homoeopaths and physicians who said they were the descendents of the Greeks. They lied to her, the whole rotten bunch, and swindled her out of thousands. It was on their strength that she refused to believe it was cancer. I sat by side of that bed one winter evening and painted her nails for her, her wasted fingers, hard as pencils in my hand. I could feel through the skin the shape of the bones like the bones of the skeleton that stood in the physiology lab at school. I had started out of a whim and out of love but I was glad when the manicuring was over.

'You have to move to a hospital,' I said.

'What for?'

'You won't get well here.'

'I will. Just wait and see.'

'You can't be cured here.' I did not have the courage to let her know that I, too, believed it was cancer.

'He will cure me.'

'Who?'

She had nodded towards the same wooden Krishna. In a sudden, boiling rage I had swept the gods and the goddesses off the table along with the bottles of nail polish. The acetone had spilled over the green carpet.

My mother had been horrified.

I switched on the light now. There was the large circular stain where the acetone had eaten away the green. I showed it to Geeta.

'It is the doing of this wooden creature,' I said pointing out the God where He played his imaginary flute.

She was bewildered by it all. I rushed her out into another room and then on to the stairs.

I stopped, breathless and flushed, at the landing, waiting for the buzzing in my head to die. She stood adjusting her sari, child of another world, traversing, like a plane at a higher altitude, a corridor separate from the dark vestibule that I had just crossed.

Watching her I was moved and I took her in my arms. Just like that. Without notice. I had done that to other women, taken them by surprise, not the surprise of a Casanova because, as one of them had explained it for me, something about the deployment and pressures of my limbs communicated that it was not that, but the pleasant, asexual surprise hug of a fellow survivor after a crash-landing. There had been many on whom I had bestowed this hug of a survivor, without another thought except the pleasure of being alive and in possession of their company: classmates, relatives, strangers — I had nearly hugged Mrs. Bedi — ayahs, librarians, nurses, aunts, friends' wives. What happened next, after the first surprise, varies. Mostly a burst of gurgling laughter, a little additional warmth to cross the Tundras of the earth, a peck on the cheek at times, and finally a pleasant disengagement. But at times there had been fiercer entanglements and this was one such because after the first gasp of surprise, Geeta clung to me. Or, maybe, it was I who did not let her go — what chance did she have against my clasp and height? But her lips were warm when I kissed her. And she let me lead her, my arm around her waist, her flanks slim and warm against mine. Thus we went up, the future Mr. and Mrs. Bhaskar, to the roof-top, where the telescope stood.

We stood in the shadow of the pill-box that housed the telescope. I asked her if she would like to see it. 'All right,' she said but I knew she wasn't interested. 'I would rather be with you,' Geeta said in a sudden burst of opening up. I had kissed her again and, trembling, hands on my shoulders, she had kissed me back. We had returned, then, into the narrow room through which I had hurried her, doubletime, past the fluteless Krishna to the upholstered safety of the Mercedez. Ten years later Geeta was the same loving, marvellous, gentle person that she had been that night. She hadn't changed except for the sudden enthusiasm for sadhus and astrologers and such like.

~

I was totally fagged out, standing at that window, looking at the bleak garden, but I hadn't the will to move. What had Geeta and Anuradha discussed at K's clinic? What would Geeta say about my efforts to get her friend into bed? I pushed the thought away; it was too complicated. Where was Anuradha's room in that mysterious haveli? Or, had she gone back to Aftab who, of course, already had that child-dancer, Azizun's niece, and, probably, Azizun herself. Quite a menage Aftab had arranged for himself.

The old man had once again appeared on the verandah of the 'house of weddings'. He was doing the last of the clearing up. He had stacked up the furniture neatly except for a high-backed chair on which he now sat. He gesticulated, occasionally, as if he talked to himself. He got up and walked slowly to the edge of the verandah where he stood still, head bowed, hands by his side. He looked as though he was reciting something. Now he lifted his arms and went through the mime of garlanding someone. I realized with amazement that it was a *jaimal* ceremony that he was going through. Fantastic, I thought. The whole city was full of nuts and not just Lal Haveli. The exchange of *jaimals* over, the old man walked briskly up to the last remaining gas light, took it down, and disappeared into the house.

~

The deal with Geeta was, more or less, closed that evening at the Maya. If I had doubts, they were not about Geeta; they concerned the deal itself, its necessity, its durability, its very idea.

Geeta was fine — as time has shown — but I had my doubts.

It was K who broke them.

The afternoon of my father's funeral, K came and threw his arm around my shoulders as though we watched not the cremation of my father but a football match. I stiffened. I was annoyed. There were hundreds of people watching. I knew he was brilliant, an F.R.C.S and much else, but didn't he have manners? Then in his deep tired voice, he said: 'I knew he would die.' And two tears rolled down his cheeks.

A little later he was gone, right out of the gates.

At dusk I came back, alone, to sit beside the pyre that would burn through the night, and, to my surprise found K on the top step, a slight, intense silhouette. He was smoking, something totally prohibited. He looked up as I approached. 'Sit down,' he said. He indicated a place as if in the vast amphitheatre of the burning grounds it was my special throne. I sat down. Outside, on the other side of the high wall, minute by minute, the traffic jammed. A hundred cars telescoped amidst a shower of abuse. We stared at the flames. 'He left you a trust,' I said, trying to compensate for my earlier petulance. 'Did he?' he said, without turning from the fire. 'He must have known I wanted to be free. I am glad he died.'

That was a hell of a thing to say. I tensed up all over again. K said, 'I did not mean it the way you imagine. And what if I did. You didn't think he was immortal? Anyway, what I meant was that he was developing melancholia.'

I looked at him uncomprehending.

'Melancholia,' he continued. 'If he had not died this morning he would have died of melancholia in a few years. In two years. Maybe three. It had been coming on ever since your mother died.'

It was this bit that I had remembered two years later while I negotiated my terms of surrender. I did not want to die of melancholia, whatever else I died of. Melancholia! For God's sake! I couldn't imagine a more ridiculous, foolish, humiliating death. I would fight it to the bitter end. And to fight I would have all the equipment. Money I already had. If it was a whore so much the better. I shall also have a wife and children and fame. Yes, fame, too. What could be a better antidote to melancholia than fame!

Fame! That bewitching siren whose song, I knew, had wrecked better ships than mine. Yet, I intended to pursue her. Better be dammed than not be mentioned at all. Fame was factual, quantitative. Almost quantitative. You knew you were first or tenth or sixteenth. There were the photographs in the newspapers and excerpts from what you said and the awed, envying, looks as men moved aside to let you pass. All this was fame.

Three months later I married Geeta.

It is a happy marriage from what anyone, including myself, can make out. I couldn't imagine life without Geeta. But, then — and here is the big question — why these little fornications? Even if I can never go to the same woman twice. It was different with Leela Sabnis but, then, she was exceptional. And, she had, or I thought she had, all the answers.

I could not stand at the window any longer. The night was too quiet, the landscape too thoughtful. For years now, I had not been at ease with such bounties of nature. God made them, people assured me, to redress the balance. Redress what balance? They did not redress any balance so far as I was concerned. To top it all, in the centre of this wasteland, stood the ghostly peepul. I shut the window and felt immediately better. I lay down on the vast bed. The coloured lights clasped me like a lover's arms, caressed me into tranquillity, nearly put me to sleep.

What of my obsession, then, obsession with women. It was not that I had not thought about the matter. I had spent money on it, a thick packet. The psychiatrists had taken the money, said a lot of things that either made too obvious a sense or no sense at all. For such a specialized profession, their command of English was particularly inadequate which led me to think the fault somehow lay with me because I so often failed to comprehend the full meaning of their disclosures. I was insecure, they said which was true but, then, who was not? I was afraid of death. That made a little more sense. I *was* mortally afraid of death. Maybe in the arms of my lovers' I found a brief respite. But, then, why didn't I go back to them? They were presumably still warm and I still had this nagging fear of cold, cold death. 'You are looking for youth,' said one of the shrinks. 'This is rubbish,' I told him. I wasn't all that old, come to think of it and none of the women were all that young. One old fellow had a different explanation. One night, after a dozen sittings, he put down his pad and pencil, made drinks for both of us. We talked of this and that, with me wondering all the time what precisely was going on. Finally, after several drinks, he said, 'You know, Mr. Bhaskar, psychiatry doesn't allow certain approaches to problems like yours. The fact, however, remains that such problems existed much before the advent of psychiatry. Certain approaches were devised at that time.'

'It is possible,' he continued, 'to conceive of this world as being populated not with people of flesh and blood, with certain sexual orientations, but with souls. You can imagine this planet humming with souls, each wanting something. Of course, many might want the same thing. A soul might also imagine that his wants, desires are best met through another soul, if that soul is the right one. That, no doubt, is a big if. Until he meets this right soul there is no peace. When you meet the right soul then, of course, things might be peaceful, may even move on towards a higher goal.'

'What goal?' I asked.

'I don't know.'

'How do you know a higher goal exists.'

'Religions would not have been so successful if such a higher goal did not exist.'

'You talk like my father,' I said.

'Well, what do you think of what I said?'

'It sounds good. One has to find a proof of the existence of souls, though.'

'Mr. Bhaskar, we assume certain things *a priori* in all exercises of logic.'

He took out a book from a shelf and read out something. It had touched me, moved me briefly to another plane. The book was by Carl Jung. I bought it later. A scatter of Jung's words passed through my head while I lay on that bed. Flying through that shower of colour, propelled by the fine smoke, I did not want to grapple with Jung.

I felt calm, hopeful. I stared at the ventilators. I did not think they would flare up again during what remained of the night. That was all for the best because I wanted now to sleep. Maybe that old shrink was right, more right than the rest of the bunch. Of course, even souls had to be governed by something. Maybe, they were governed by Freud's stuff. Maybe by something else. Maybe by both.

But what if nothing like a soul at all existed? What if nothing existed that could not be reasoned through as old Leela insisted?

Walking this same beach, scholar Leela said I suffered from delusions. Maybe she was right. At some point on the horizon all mixed up. You can call things by any name you choose.

~

Dr. Leela Sabnis, a professor, descendant of a long line of professors, M.A. and Ph.D. from Michigan, something else from London, short, shapely, small-breasted, skinny, trained in philosophy, emancipator of women, married and divorced, believer in free love, harbinger of a new order of things, reformer of the body and a mechanic of the spirit, a good lover.

We met on a Sunday afternoon on the lawns of a seaside hotel. After several beers, the voids beating upon me in a thick bombardment, K and I sat, watching the spate of tourists and their assorted bikinis. Prof. Sabnis came up: Jeans, slippers, navy-blue T-shirt, hair pulled back in a pony-tail from the smooth intelligent brow.

'Hello,' she said to K. K invited her to sit down. We ordered a beer for her. For a reformer old Leela could be surprisingly quiet. And quiet she stayed that afternoon smoking cigarettes, crossing and uncrossing her legs, adjusting her pony-tail. K told me to drop her home. On the way, I asked her what she did.

'I teach,' she said. 'And you?'

'I make plastics.'

'Buckets?'

'Also buckets.'

She nodded and lit a cigarette.

'What do you teach?' I said.

'Philosophy.'

'That is just what I need.'

We laughed, fell silent. The Sunday crowds filled the streets. They were thick along the sea. Ice cream trolleys, *chaatwalahs*. Girls from Bandra jostled by the boys, giggling, white teeth in dark mouths. Skirts had grown shorter that year and have been growing shorter ever since.

Leela lived in an apartment in a block of apartments. Would I like to come up for coffee, she said.

I didn't want the coffee and I didn't want to go up but the voids were upon me, pulling and pushing, and Geeta was at Ooty with the children. I said: 'Yes, I would like some coffee.'

Leela Sabnis was a scholar, an educator's child, much as I was a scientist's. She could read at three and she hadn't stopped, from what I could make out. She knew Marathi, Sanskrit, French and German besides English, Hindi and Tamil. The last she had picked up during the seven year posting of her husband at Madras, as an executive of an oil company.

That flat of hers is not far from here. Two rooms, maybe three. Crammed with books. Books on the floor, books against the walls, on the toilet, inside the laundry bag, on the bed. The first time we made love, I had to remove a dozen books from the bed while she undressed. If I had been muddled by the voids, books had done the job for Leela Sabnis. Her husband, she claimed proudly, divorced her for reading too much. He did the right thing, for all I know. But I am not fair — to Leela or her books. There were little gems strewn about those ten tons of printed paper. I picked up a large assortment, like a child let loose in a toy shop. I stuffed my pockets with them, stuffed my mouth, my nose, my eyes. Then the voids returned, knocked them out of my hands, emptied my pockets, made me rinse my month with their bitter gall. Some, though, have stuck even if I can't make much sense out of them.

Leela Sabnis liked to sit deep in her emerald sofa. Behind her stood the philosophers of America and Europe. Freud as well, bearded and saintly, indefatigable, groping in the night of man's mind, strewn with piss and excreta, struggling to put man together, the pervert and the insane, but also those who, whole otherwise, walked the beaches at night and cried for the spirit. Leela Sabnis was an explorer, trained in Michigan in the tools of exploring. But Michigan was crumbling; the West itself was crumbling; in Vietnam and Detroit and the by-ways of New York. Where did that leave her?

Also, behind Leela Sabnis, stood the reformers, the saints of her own civilization. Whatever had happened to them? Who spoke, they or Michigan, when Leela said, 'I am concerned about you, luv.'

I shall never know. Leela Sabnis was a muddled creature. As muddled as me. Muddled by her ancestry, by marriage, by divorce, by too many books. When she made love — yes, we had got around to it soon after — when she made love, the confusion momentarily lifted. But immediately after, as she stood smoking, looking down at me — little bare feet on the stone floor, small breasts just a little sweaty — as she stood there looking down at me, the confusion descended in one roaring storm. Her first words would be 'Let me being where I left off.' And she would begin where she had left off, reeling off diagnoses, half sense, half poppycock, too much analysis.

Leela Sabnis had obsessions. She had an obsession for explanations. Like my father. What led to what. Causes and effects. Effects and effects. What made people tick. The neat kingdoms of reason.

'I am not fond of you,' she told me one evening. 'That would be lying, but I am concerned, I am worried. Tell me, what makes you tick?'

'The voids,' I said without enthusiasm.

'The voids? What voids?'

'I hear this song way up in the sky. All the time.'

'What song?'

'I want; I want; I want.'

'I want. I want. I want. Just like that?'

'Yes.'

Leela Sabnis, braless, taut thighed, shook her head. Besides, I had begun to wonder what made her tick.

Leela Sabnis analysed too much. She analysed like other people breathe. If we are talking of compulsions, there was a woman who had a compulsion — to talk, to analyse. There was nothing that she could not work out through cool analysis: the universe, the living and the dead, worlds seen and unseen. 'All this is very well,' she would say in answer to my lamentations about the voids. 'Not irrelevant, but not very relevant either. It is too general, vague, too mystical. What we need is detail, data.' 'I do not say it will be easy to get the data,' she would add, drying the moisture under the folds of her breasts, 'but we are lucky in the tools that have now been put in our hands. If man can go to the moon, surely he can make a dent in understanding himself. Even if he cannot grapple with the whole of himself, he can at least make a dent. What can you do with mysticism? Take it or leave it. What good is a doctrine that says: take me or leave me, do not analyse me. It is Descartes that you need to understand, Som Bhaskar.'

She would be dressed by this time. Slacks and *churidars* set her off. Hair loose, without make-up, she could have passed for one of her students. She was definitely skinny. It was only saris — chiffons, silks — that made her look the woman she was. And a beautiful one. In the pale chiselled face the breeding stood out. There was intelligence in the large brown eyes, touched a little with eye-shadow — she had her vanity. But there was also confusion, kept back, but very much there, not yet analysed.

She would be dressed and outside the french windows the beach would be dark, and sufficiently cool, for us to step out.

Mrs. Sabnis on my arm, we would go out into the dark evenings, along the sea, barefoot, on the wet, spongy sand. On the whole, she was no pedagogue, no name-dropper. She had ideas of her own that she catapulted with singular ferocity, charging them with the electricity of her brain. You couldn't say she hadn't worked at her thoughts. She had slogged. She had studied and understood and memorized. Oh yes, Leela Sabnis knew a lot even if she had experienced little and suffered even less.

In the dark, walking along the line of the surf, her waist supple under my hand, I gloried in her chatter, her chatter mostly of me, what was the matter with me. 'A man so successful, so intelligent, why should such a man so confused,' she would say striding the sand.

Ah, my Leela Sabnis, how little you understood the roots of the world's confusion.

'Tell me!' I would ask her. 'What do you think is the matter with me?'

'You are much too high strung. Without reason. You are a neurotic. A compulsive fornicator.'

'Thanks.'

'You are always playing games with the world.'

'Who is not?'

'You are playing games even now. You must be serious and try to listen to me. You are lonely on the one hand. On the other, you have built a shell around yourself. To protect yourself.'

'Protect against what?'

'Against your feelings of inadequacy.'

'The shell business sounds awful.'

'You are still not serious. You are not listening to me. Don't you agree with me?'

'About the shell?'

'You are bored, bored stiff in your little shell. That is the long and the short of it.'

'Isn't that a little too short?'

She would ignore me, 'And you are only thirty. Just imagine!' She would look at me with sudden concern, even affection, and it made me feel sorry that I caused her such concern.

Wondering, curious, analysing, correlating, getting nowhere. She tried to help me reason things through but I got nowhere. And when you get nowhere you get vengeful, angry, all the more querulous with that someone who put you on the planet in the first place.

She had her prescription: Descartes.

'Descartes?'

'Yes, Descartes. He explained it all a long time ago.'

'I think, therefore, I am?'

'Yes.'

'But is that really so?'

'What else?'

'What of intuitions? Of faith?'

'You cannot have intuition or faith in what you cannot think through.'

'What of the world of the soul?'

'That, too, can be reasoned through, Descartes separated matter from spirit. The soul, too, has to be reasoned through.'

I thought of Spinoza in the streets of Amsterdam, grinding lenses for a living. He was a proud man, a man my father admired.

'What about Spinoza?'

'What about him?'

'Didn't he say both matter and spirit embraced in God, and flowed from Him?'

'That is bullshit.'

'Bravo!' I would say, my hands on her narrow shoulders, twisting her around until I could kiss her. 'Bravo!'

Leela Sabnis fascinated me. For a while, I had believed in the powers of her cures. And yet, when I left her, with the usual two books that I borrowed every time we met, when I left her, a thirty year old shell, what I heard in the twilight was not the wisdom of Descartes, or the hum of the evening traffic, or the bulletlike whistling past of the suburban trains, not the whine of the ubiquitous jet heading for Santa Cruz, what I heard was not these but the strumming of great chords way up in the sky, beating the old tattoo: I want. I want. I want.

Leela and I did not exactly break off. After six months our affair fizzled out. We met, talked, horsed around but didn't particularly want to get into bed. Leela, of course, had her reasoned explanation. In the world of matter we had fed on sex and now we were satiated. In the world of the spirit we still enjoyed conversation. The two worlds, by her lights, did not meet, could not meet.

Maybe, *that* was why we fell apart. What I needed, perhaps, was something, somebody, somewhere in which the two worlds combined.

My eyes went to the peacock on the carpet. He seemed to stare right into my eyes. Hypnotized by its glance, wafted on the spectrum of the rainbow, I finally fell asleep.

And I dreamt I was in a labyrinth. The walls of the caverns were damp, the ceiling low. I was alone. Then Anuradha joined me. She wore a petticoat and a blouse. I asked her, 'What is in the last labyrinth, Anuradha?'

She laughed. 'If you want to sleep with me it is all right by me,' she said.

She dropped her petticoat. I lay on top of her. I woke up feeling moist, sticky, roused. I lay while wondering where I was. The colour in the ventilators was slowly dissolving. In a couple of hours I had to catch my plane.

~

Anuradha saw me off on the driveway. She looked just as she did when she had left me. I wondered if she had slept at all.

Aftab, she said, was asleep.

'Of course.'

'Give my regards to Geeta.'

'I will.'

'Don't go away in anger.'

'Good bye,' I said.

The plane circled the city before setting its bearings. Amidst the white-washed houses, the temples and the mosques raised their heads in the morning sun. Everything looked hot and prostrate. There was the river with its decrepit, world famous water front. On the other bank, somewhere amidst those trees, I knew, was Gargi's cottage. I was in a hurry to get back to Bombay, back to my factories, Mr. Thapar would, from now on, handle Aftab. The past twenty four hours had been like a dream. And I was glad the dream was over.

8

K, according to my father, was a man for all seasons. In age he was closer to me than to my father but he had maintained a distance and a reserve with me which became apparent only when we were left alone. I was surprised, therefore, when he phoned me at the office and invited me to lunch.

Over coffee, his eyes narrowed against the glare of the harbour, he said, 'I understand you visited Aftab Rai.'

'Why, yes,' I said. 'Who told you?'

'Anuradha was here.'

'I see.'

'She said you are after Aftab's company.'

'What of it?'

'He is an odd sort.'

'It takes all kinds to make the world.'

K did not smile.

'And that is an odd sort of a house, that haveli of his.'

'Have you been there?'

'Yes. Aftab invited your father once...'

'Oh, did he? I didn't know.'

'Yes, he did. For a meal. It appeared — well, a depraved sort of a place to me.'

I thought of the diamond on Aftab's little toe.

'I should have thought so,' I laughed.

'What did you think of it?'

'It was quaint.'

'You will be going there again?'

'Why not? I am over twenty one, you know.'

'I know.'

We fell silent. A monkey-man sought our attention from the pavement below. For five rupees his monkeys would have showed us some sexual tricks. A knot of junkies, gaunt, their hair matted, passed by as though sleep-walking. There wasn't much in Aftab's haveli that was not available within a hundred yards of where we sat.

The lunch came to an abrupt end. K started to say something, then pulled himself up. He looked at his watch. 'I had better run along. It's May Day today. They are bound to bring in casualties.'

'Can I come with you?'

'Sure.'

Outside, it was hot and sultry. I said, 'An odd couple, no doubt.'

'Aftab and Anuradha?'

He made them sound like the indestructible organic compounds that my factories churned out day and night.

'Yes.'

'I suppose so.'

'What do you know about them, anyway?' I said.

He did not answer. For the remaining half-mile to his clinic we drove in silence.

A constable was waiting for him along with a dark thin man. The man had a deep gash along one cheek. The blood ran down his face and into the collar of his shirt. He was barefoot.

'Are you a worker?' K asked him as he got ready to stitch the wound.

'No. I don't have a job,' said the man.

'What rally were you in? Raise your hand if you feel the needle.'

'You know,' the man said, 'you know, in Cambodia they tear children apart. Children of the officers of the old government. They don't waste bullets on them. The officers are killed with bayonets or clubs. The women, too. Their wives, of course. They have killed ten lakhs by now. Another twenty might have to be finished before the new order can be established. They take them out into the country in trucks. They make the men strip and kneel, their hands tied behind their backs. Two men bayonet them simultaneously, one in the chest, the other in the back. Their families are looking on all the while. You know what they have been doing to the women? They...'

'Shut up,' K shouted in a sudden rage. 'Just shut up.'

The man clammed up at once, a picture of obedience. K had a way of exercising authority if he chose to. I wondered if I really knew him as well as I imagined.

When the man was gone, K lit a cigarette and sat back. 'You asked me what I know about them?'

I took a second to catch on. 'Well, yes.'

'Not much about Aftab. A little more about Anuradha. She used to be a film star.'

'When did you meet her?'

'Oh, many years ago, quite by accident. At the bedside, in fact, of an actress who lived in the flat next to mine. The actress was dying — of liquor, I think. There was very little to be done. She was there along with an old man.'

'Well?'

'What I remember most about her is that she wouldn't let me leave. She was terrified. After the actress died, I brought her over to my flat for some brandy. We talked a bit. She is odd, as you say. She was odd even then but I liked her a lot. She didn't like being in the movies.'

K picked up a stack of X-rays, put them, one by one, against the light. An ambulance, white and gleaming, backed out of the green gates of the hospital across the street. My mother had been hospitalized there until she ran away one night. Painters were putting a new coat on the gate.

'Was that the last you saw of her?' I said.

K did not reply. He was not much of a conversationalist and I knew he couldn't be rushed. I sensed, however, a new reluctance in him. I let him finish the X-rays, then repeated the question.

'I saw her off and on, went to a couple of her parties. She had an aunt living at Juhu. I even saw her shoot one whole morning. Then she went away with Aftab.' He fell silent again, lit another cigarette, became thoughtful. 'A strange thing happened a few years later. One night, Aftab phoned from Benaras. He was very upset. He had just been told that Anuradha was very ill and could I go and see her at her aunt's place. I didn't know Aftab but I liked Anuradha and I went. It was past midnight. I had to wake up the aunt. She was surprised to see me. Anuradha had had an attack of small pox, she said, which was serious enough, but she was not aware of any sudden developments. We went to her room. It was locked from inside. We had to break it down. Anuradha lay in the tub in the bathroom. She had cut her wrists.'

'Good God!' I said, horrified.

Slowly, another point sank into me.

'But how did Aftab know about it if her aunt did not?'

'That remains a mystery.'

As I drove back to the office I could not shake her thought away. I saw her sitting on the divan holding my face in her hands and, then, slumped in the brown water, her body covered with scabs, blood pumping steadily out of her slashed wrists. I felt sick, nauseated.

What had my lunch with K been about? Depravity? Maybe it was depravity that had so stirred me that night. All in all, though, I had no desire to return to the labyrinths of Lal Haveli. The cutting edge of my life pointed the other way, even if I did not know *which* other way. Anuradha's cold farewell had put an end to my obsession with her. It was time now to turn to the affairs at hand, the wrapping up of Aftab's company, in the interest not only of business but also of the forces of evolution, the survival of the fittest.

~

I had nearly forgotten Aftab and his haveli. If I had met him at a party I would have ignored him. And, yet, when he came and sat near me at the next meeting of the Plastic Manufacturers Association, touching my hand with his own, bringing with him that peculiar musty fragrance of his haveli's interiors, that must surely have existed only on that one spot on earth, I felt my breath quicken, my thoughts coming suddenly to a boil. Images, drenched in the colours of bangles, smothered my senses. While the minister humbugged a hundred businessmen, I could only hear the songs of Azizun, the footwork of the little dancer, the sound of my nail tracing the line of a vase etched in marble. Echoes of those empty rooms shot about my head like billiard balls. My senses knocked at the brown teak doors of a room in which the carpet with a peacock's image lay. I dared not open that door. And yet, even before the vote of thanks, when Aftab whispered, 'Come with me, there is a plane at five,' I went.

Benaras was hot. Tarakki had brought the Dodge. I noticed the wistfulness with which Aftab watched the goings on beyond the tinted glass, like an animal in a cage. My eyes met Tarakki's in the rear view mirror. I looked away.

Spurred by the heat, Tarakki drove fast, as fast as the crowds allowed. The river had thinned down as had the rush of pilgrims. There were traffic lights at wide intervals. Each one of them was red but Tarakki, swearing under his breath, ran through them all.

In fact, it was not to Aftab's house that we went that evening. I found myself recording each crossing, each turning, as though I were being kidnapped and would later have to find my way back. The streets widened or narrowed without explanation. Tyres squealing, the car reversed direction. There were trees and long stretches of cobblestones. At one point, we stopped to let a procession of ash-smeared sadhus pass. Silent, except for the jangling of their *chimtas*, unblinking eyes straight ahead, they passed like a pageant of ghosts, grey and ephemeral against the white houses. Sometime later, we stopped. I had been able to retain nothing of the route.

It was nearly dark. I followed Aftab out of the car. He walked up a little distance and beckoned. His manner suggested a secret rendezvous. What I saw, at the turn of the corner, however, was a vast *chowk* afloat with *rehris*. Each of the *rehris* had an acetylene light. They were packed like sampans in Hongkong. On the layers of dust and stench of rotten fruit lay fumes of acetylene. A large crowd milled about the *rehris*.

'Our summers are long and hot,' Aftab said. 'But it would rain sooner or later.' He pointed towards the sky as if the rain lurked somewhere behind the stars.

He stood for a moment, pensive and watchful. Then he stepped into the crowd. His step was firm. He walked without touching anyone as though he abhorred contact. Yet he was happy, buoyant, as I had seldom seem him. The *rehris* were loaded with knick-knacks: plastic, rayon fabrics, smuggled shirts from Nepal, tobacco, eatables, pornography, soda water, religious books. Indifferent to the heat, the crowd jostled about in the highest of spirits. Here and there, in the wavering light, the face of a pretty woman stood out. There was something about them, the women, a coquettish consent, a readiness for romance, that intrigued me.

'There is a festival today,' Aftab said. Maybe that explained it. At the far end of the square Aftab pointed out the silhouette of a dark mysterious shrine.

'They used to perform human sacrifice there,' he announced. 'Azizun lives over there,' he added in the same breath as though she too had something to do with human sacrifice.

And where was Anuradha? At Aftab's haveli? In the streets nearby? In a dargah? That morning in Bombay, shaving in the brightly tiled bathroom of the town apartment in which I then lived, I had thought of her. It was the sight of an iron grill, ornate and delicate, in an apartment across the street, that had sparked her memory. The apartment belonged to an acquaintance, chief of a pharmaceutical company, and I had seen the grill many times before. I had even touched it, traced the iron vines and leaves. But in the pre-dawn darkness, in the diffused light from the sky and the sea, it had been transformed, filled with a life of its own, until it stood detached from the building; stood breathing over the balcony like a black mysterious animal. Why it should have brought on the memories of Anuradha, I do not know. After I finished shaving I stood for a while at the window, looking at the grill and building all around. There was a mystery about Anuradha that I had yet to crack. She should have been no more to me than a woman trying to save her lover's (husband's?) property. She should have been transparent. Why should she appear mysterious unless, possibly, there was a mystery within me that, in her proximity, got somehow stirred, as one tuning fork might stir another.

So, while Geeta thought I was getting ready, I stood at the bathroom window wondering about the mystery of the grill and that other mystery, the mystery of Anuradha. In the half-dawn the concrete all around me loomed all the more overwhelming. No wonder I had not noticed the grill all these years. Perhaps my father was right. The concrete did change your vision, narrowed down the wavelengths of sight and sound and thought that you could register. Aftab's haveli, his city, transmitted different wavelengths and appeared mysterious because I could not receive their messages.

Beyond a faint crackle, that is. It was the crackle, that was important. Without it, I would not have known the existence of another world.

'I thought you were getting ready.'

Geeta had come in from the bedroom.

'There is still time.' I put an arm around her waist. She was slim and shapely and, at that hour, very desirable. Yet, lately, we had not been particularly active in that department.

'It is a meeting of the Association?'

'Yes.'

'You will be meeting Aftab?'

'I guess so.'

'I hope you are not getting too involved with him.'

'Has K been talking to you?'

'Yes. I have my own feelings, too.'

'Anyway, I am not getting involved with him.'

'But you are going ahead with the acquisition of his company.'

'That is another matter.'

After a silence she had said, 'I hope you won't go off to Benaras, like the last time.'

'Of course not.'

And, yet, here I was, admiring coquettish women and places of human sacrifice and now entering a narrow lane that presumably led to Azizun's place.

Despite the heat, the lane was full. Of men, women and animals. The women were probably wives of workers and clerks doing their buying at the shops that occupied the ground floors of the buildings on either side. They could not care less what went on the floors above. Or, maybe, as in Bombay, there was a magical hour when the ordinary life of these lanes instantly yielded to a life of flaming passions, madness, and suicides. Four Nepali girls, their *kamizes* tight around their hips stepped giggling out of a photographer's shop. They stopped abruptly before Aftab, took a quick glance at me and went away, giggling once again. We entered the dim hallway of a house. A mongrel, its coat covered with scabs, lay curled in its cool darkness. From Aftab he received a sharp, unexpected kick in the belly and ran away screaming. We went up the steep stairs.

We came upon an unlit landing, passed through a creaky unbolted door and entered a courtyard. It was in fact the roof of the shop below. Its hot brick was sprinkled with water and gave off an odour of wet earth. Beyond the courtyard, Aftab knocked on a wooden door. It was opened by a middle aged woman. She was respectful but did not smile. 'Azizun Jan?' Aftab enquired in his soft, hesitant voice, the fine eyebrows (I wondered if he plucked them) raised just a little. The woman nodded. We followed her at a distance. 'She is Azizun's mother.' After a pause he added, 'Some hooligans cut off her breasts during the riots of 1947.'

'Good God.'

'She was among the finest singers of the city.'

'Does she still sing?'

Aftab looked at me in disbelief, annoyance. 'Would you sing if your breasts were cut off?'

I had never seen him out of countenance before. He opened a door and peered. The sound of *ghunghrus* spilled out.

'Let her teach,' said Aftab, quickly shutting the door. He led me to a decrepit wooden balcony that overlooked the street. Or, maybe, the wooden planks hid a steel frame. The bannister, in any case, was of wood. Under my hands it felt of dust and flaking paint. A couple of flower pots stood to one side. They smelled of wet earth, too, and of marigolds. The way Aftab bent down and smelt them I had a feeling they were his gifts to the house. Across us, at eye level, was a tenement similar to Azizun's. A man and a woman stood looking down. I could see right through the tunnel of rooms at the end of which an *angithi* belched smoke through a mound of coals. On the third floor stood two plump girls, also looking down. 'I have always suffered from vertigo,' said Aftab pulling back a bit. 'Can you look down and tell me who is making all that racket?'

In the street below bedlam prevailed. It was like a river of bobbing heads in spate. Smoke arose from a hundred *angithis.* Radios blared. The complexion of the crowd had subtly changed. The housewives had retired, their place taken by young men in a variety of dress. They had black glossy hair and a raucous laugh. There was a strange similarity about them as if they had been cloned from the same movie star. I wondered what they did for a living. In Bombay, I would have known but here I was at a loss. Their muscular bodies and white flashing teeth exuded mountains of unconsumed energy that would doubtless explode in a hundred ways before the night was done. To the right of me, before the mirror-doors of a cinema, two young men horsed around watched by a circle of admirers. That was the racket that Aftab had referred to. One of the men wore a bright red shirt, the other a green scarf. 'Two young men are horsing around,' I informed him, but even as I talked, I realized that the 'horsing around' had turned into a full-scale fight. The friendly yelling had turned into grunts of wild rage. A couple of bystanders stepped in, making gestures of peace but, just then, the red shirt flashed what looked like a knife and plunged it into the other's stomach. I could see green-scarf holding the hilt of the dagger, trying to pull it out. Red-shirt sped through the crowd on bare feet. Green-scarf fell on the pavement and the crowd closed over him.

'Somebody has been stabbed,' I shouted to Aftab. What with the heat, I wanted to be sick.

'What?'

'Stabbed.'

'Oh, God.'

The crowd grew by the second. There was no sign either of a policeman or a doctor. The smoke grew thicker, the radios louder. And, now, Aftab put a trembling hand on my arm. 'Is he dead?' he asked in a voice shaken with panic, his hand damp against my arm.

'I don't think he is dead — yet.' At that moment, they started to put him in the back of a tonga. Aftab was now looking down, his vertigo forgotten.

'They are putting the poor bastard in a tonga! The jogging is not going to help his pain.'

Aftab still clutched my arm but there was a new fascination in his voice that went beyond the usual fascination that attracts people to an accident. For a long moment, he stood riveted to the spot, one hand on my arm, the other clutching the rotting bannister.

'Let us go in,' he said finally when the tonga had disappeared.

We entered now the room in which the dance practice was still going on. Azizun sat, her legs to one side, singing. Beside her, sat the pair of musicians whom I had seen in Aftab's haveli the other night. An old fan churned the hot air overhead. The two girls, Azizun's pupils, were dressed in *churidars* and frock. The frocks might have been part of a school uniform. They were not more than ten or eleven. I wondered where Aftab's young lover was, the girl who had danced at the haveli that night. The girls did not look up as we entered. Azizun smiled brightly, her fine teeth very white between the coarse lips, then went back to her singing. We sat down on a threadbare carpet that had been spread along a wall. It was a shabby little place but the activity of the children relieved it. I did not know much about dance but I knew they were good at whatever they were doing. You could see this on their faces and on the faces of their teachers. The girls did not either have the upper garments of a kathak dancer or did not want to spoil what they had. Their frocks, made of thin cotton, ballooned as they twirled about. Their arms were slender, perhaps, undernourished. Once of them, I now understood was Radha, the other Krishna. So, here too Krishna ruled. Why couldn't they put into dance the problems of people like me? Weren't there masters who could work out the choreography of my lust for Anuradha unless they considered the love of Radha and Krishna to include all loves, all lusts, all disappointments. The girls now moved into an intricate spell of footwork. It lasted a long time, their feet hollow and sharp by turn on the cement floor. How could anyone go through those manoeuvres on half-rations. Aftab slept, a cigarette dangling from his lips. The footwork had gone awry and Azizun cut in. The girls stopped. They were disappointed. Perspiration poured down their small oval faces. Again they began, getting derailed even sooner. They wiped their faces with the ends of their frocks. They looked unhappy, angry with themselves. They were exhausted and breathless. They probably needed rest. Why were they doing what they were doing? My daily expenses were perhaps more than what was spent on them in a month. Was it this gap that they hoped to bridge with their footwork? What gap *could* you bridge on an empty stomach, anyway? The well-fed will never be beaten by the hungry, old Leela used to say, unless hunger itself became the weapon. They started again. Maybe it was something else that drove them, some other hunger, more powerful than the hunger of the body, something closer to the kind of hunger I suffered from. If they did, they were certainly showing greater perseverance than I had.

The music ended and, with its end, noises of the street flowed freely into the little room. The shouting and the screaming seemed all the more insane because I did not think anything was getting done down there. The noise of radios and whirling tonga-wheels dominated all, as if a chariot race was on. From a distance came reports of firecrackers as a groom, perhaps, set out for his bride. Somewhere close by a conch was blown, over and over.

Azizun brought in a tray of some sherbet with dirty looking ice. She sat around, shy and silent, while we sipped at it. It was too sweet and fuelled my nausea but I dared not leave it for the fear of upsetting her. In her own little home, with her mutilated mother, she appeared much more defenceless than I had given her credit for. In the bright light of the room, her mouth and eyes showed their vulnerability. She wore a *garara* of light blue linen. Her dupatta climbed continually to her throat revealing the fullness of her bosom. She was younger than I had thought.

The girls came back. They had powdered their dark faces and one of them carried a doll against her talcumed cheeks. Aftab got up and went out of the door, probably to the toilet.

'You have a nice house,' I said to Azizun by way of small talk.

'All these houses belong to Seth Sahib.' She waved in the direction of the street.

'What Seth Sahib? Aftab?'

'Yes. His father had them built. We have lived here a long time. Gargi Mata lives upstairs. Have you met her?'

I tried to place the name.

'She is the daughter of the sufi.'

I got it now.

'I have seen her,' I said.

So it wasn't a cock-and-bull story after all.

'You have a room at the haveli?' I asked her.

'Yes. I stay the night there whenever I am required.'

'Has he bought you?' I asked foolishly, irritably.

I was annoyed with Aftab for having brought me out on this excursion.

'He treats you like a slave?' I persisted.

'No.'

'Of course he does. Before you it was Anuradha. I suppose he treated her like a slave too.'

She looked horrified. 'He worships her,' she said.

'Don't be silly.'

Azizun shut up. The girls watched us wondering, probably, what a strange quarrelsome man was visiting them.

'He *worships* Anuradha?' I asked.

She nodded gravely and something about her manner made me wonder if she meant it literally.

'What do you mean?'

In reply she pointed towards the fan.

'The fan?'

She burst out laughing. 'I don't know. I don't know. Can I sing for you?'

'I like your singing very much but first tell me: Who is Anuradha, anyway?'

Azizun's reaction was not one that I might have expected from one of Anuradha's rivals. She was distinctly deferential, awed, as if I had asked her to inform on a great personage. It was almost as bad as if I had said, 'Who the hell is Krishna?'

She started to say something when Aftab entered.

'While we are here let us go and meet Gargi,' he said, with uncharacteristic briskness. He bade Azizun a quick salaam. I, too, said my good bye.

The girls watched us shyly, the younger chewed the doll's hair. I patted their little dark heads telling them to 'keep it up'. When we stepped out on the landing, I said to Aftab, 'I really admire the perseverance of those girls.'

'I know you admire that sort of thing,' he said.

'Don't you?'

'Not at all.'

As we climbed the next flight of steps, Aftab turned conspiratorial, paused every few steps, and amidst the odour of bats and beetle-spit, asked me if I had heard of Gargi. I said I had, sort of. I reminded him of the trip across the Ganga. He shook his head, as if he had a headache — which, indeed, he might have had considering that my own head was splitting — but explained nothing besides adding with a wry smile, 'This, too, is a labyrinth, my friend.'

There was a door with a sign in vermilion on one side of it. After a moment it was opened by Gargi. I recognized her. She gave us the same radiant smile and let us in.

Gargi led us into a squarish room. Its stained glass ventilators were surprisingly like the ones at Aftab's haveli. The room was bare except for a pitcher and mats along one corner. A young girl — the one who had held the lantern for the *mallah* — brought us glasses of cold water from the pitcher. As soon as we were seated, Aftab broke into a spate of words. He sounded like a sullen schoolboy but Gargi listened to him with attention. Occasionally, she smiled or gestured. She had the most gentle and engaging smile of anybody I had ever known. I wanted to hug her when she smiled. Aftab talked of so many things at once that I could not make out what bothered him the most. It was all grief, of one kind or another, how his business was going downhill, and Azizun was not keeping well, and the haveli an the care were crumbling down. There was none of the reserve that I had always associated with him. He told her of the stabbing that had occurred in the street below. The tenants were bothering him, he said, but he avoided them for the fear that he too might be stabbed. Gargi looked at him reprimandingly. Then he started to talk about me: 'a great businessman from Bombay', etc. He mentioned how my touch could turn mud into gold and how happy I must be to have no problems in life. Gargi gave me a knowing smile.

'The problem lies in the stars,' said Aftab. 'We become what our stars make us.' Gargi raised her eyebrows heavenwards in mock commiseration but didn't say a word. I had not yet heard her speak.

There was some kind of a bond between Gargi and Aftab and I wondered what it was. Gargi, of course, was the daughter of the sufi, but was that all? In any event, there was a great deal of affection between the two, the kind that exists between a sister and a brother.

I sat with my back to the door and it was her perfume that I first recognized. I stiffened, my heart beating a little wilder, my throat dry but I did not turn to look at her. It might have been a one-shot obsession but at that moment, while she hesitated at the doorstep, I knew I was in love with her. Gargi was looking at her over my head and Anuradha moved now — softly. She did not have her usual high heels. She touched Gargi's feet and sat down next to me. 'I did not know your were in Benaras,' she said.

'Well, here I am.'

She smiled, composed, fully in control. Aftab, who had taken no notice of her, now started to speak again. Gargi let him talk without interruption although her face easily reflected her reaction if there was something to react to. At one point she took a pad and a pencil from under the mat, wrote something on it and passed it on to Anuradha. I wondered if she was under a vow of silence. And, then, suddenly, it struck me that Gargi was a deaf-mute. I had no doubt in my mind, no second thoughts. I had no doubts because I had seen her before, walking silently about the darkness of my dreams. That is why, entering the room, I had felt at home with her. And, I was positive she knew me, too. She understands, I said to myself, the only one who understands. And, was it this flat of Gargi's and not the fan, that Azizun had indicated when we were talking of Anuradha? Did Aftab really worship Anuradha? I looked at the two of them with a new curiosity.

In her note she had asked Anuradha to bring me some khir which Anuradha now did. In spite of my nausea I ate it. Everyone fell silent and watched me eat. It was as though a delinquent son, hungry and worn, had returned home. When I was finished with the first helping, Anuradha brought me another. I finished half of it. Then set it down. 'I feel very full,' I said apologetically. 'I shouldn't have accepted it.'

Gargi smiled. I wondered if she could read my lips well enough. I added more slowly, 'I am sorry.'

'Never mind,' Anuradha said, 'I shall finish it.'

She ate slowly and, as she always did, with a peculiar concentration. Occasionally, she glanced up, keeping track of the conversation. I talked to Gargi, telling her of how good the khir was, and how my mother made sweets at home when I was a boy. I told her about how she developed cancer, preferred Krishna to medicines, and died. I told her about my father, his preoccupation towards the end. I talked carefully, modulating my lips. I was very keen that Gargi should understand me. And then, suddenly, in the middle of a sentence, I became aware of the charge that had gradually built up between me and Anuradha. It was like the exchange that had occurred in the dargah and then, again, in the Blue Room. This time, I knew, it had something to do with the act of sharing that bit of khir. I stumbled to a stop, my words choked off by a rush of emotion. I stared into Anuradha's eyes. One moment there was puzzlement in the brown irises, then they were filled with understanding and finally with confusion. Blood rose to her face. She emptied the bowl and put it down. I looked around. Gargi was smiling at me as before, waiting for me to continue. But I was certain she had understood everything. She had understood not only what had happened just then but also all that had taken place between us in the dargah, on the banks of the Ganga, in the Blue Room, in the Intercontinental Hotel, and, in any other place under the sun.

~

It was late when we left Gargi's place. The photographer's shop was closed. Of the stabbing no traces remained — not even in the person of an odd policeman. I didn't think human life counted for very much on that street. It had been a strange evening. I should have been back in Bombay, asleep beside Geeta on the wide bed. Instead... instead what?

Instead, Aftab led us towards the end of the street. A holy bull, a bell around his neck, blocked the way. He looked up at me smugly as I detoured around his head. Beyond the bull there was a hint of the river. On a deserted *ghat* some kind of a carnival was on. There were flags and petromax lights and the sound of drums. There was the cackle of vendors. A beggar tried to grab my feet. I kicked at him — to the horror of the bystanders.

There was a juggler, tall, broad-shouldered, bare-chested, virile. He wore the narrow brocaded black waistcoat of the gypsies and a black *lungi*. His eyes were coal-black, a little drugged. He laid them out now, a dozen balls, sticks, copper wire, china plates, a jagged piece of glass. He performed faultlessly with the balls, his eyes not straying from Anuradha's face for a minute. The longing in them was so obvious that I wondered how she could ignore it. Aftab threw him coins. And now the rest of his family, the rope dancers, the drummers, swept into the act. The drumming was stepped up. The mother took up a song that brought forth the sands of Arabia. It was as though a desert had suddenly sprung on the banks of the Ganga.

A tight-rope was now slung between two sets of poles. A boy and a girl, probably brother and sister, moved from either end of the rope to meet at the centre, under the light of a petromax. Locked in an incestuous embrace, they danced about in jerky motions. As a finale, the boy stood on the father's shoulders, the girl sat on the boy's. This grotesque of rags and sores now moved towards us with a cripple's gait, the light for a moment darkened by its menacing shadow. I handed them money before they could pester Anuradha but they went to her anyway. The juggler grinned at her and she smiled back. She opened her purse and took out a couple of notes. She raised her hand in the air towards the girl who, in slow movements, bent down from her brother's shoulders, the little human pyramid shaking all the time, and took the money from her hand.

There was a flower stall where Aftab bought a *gajra* for Anuradha. We waited while he put it in her hair. There was a stall of funny mirrors, another, for Siamese twins. A second juggler put a long needle through his cheeks. A clown with a picture machine sang: '*Kutub Sahib ki laat ko dekho, aur Duke Connaught ko dekho.*' An old man sitting on a stool, all by himself, in a voice of unbelievable sadness, sang a Bhojpuri ballad. Entranced, for some reason unable to control my emotions, I stood before him aware neither of Anuradha nor of the carnival nor of my bearings. I was only aware that I stood far from home, in a most desolate of places, from where there could be no rescue. When Aftab offered the old man money he refused. A yogi stood in the centre of a little crowd, the point of a spear against an eye. As we watched the spear started to bend, slowly at first, then in a rush until the looplit fell on the ground. The crowd applauded.

In a tent a dancer, looking a bit like Azizun, waited, hand on hips. Anuradha paused before an astrologer's stall, hesitated, then went in. We followed.

The stall was dimly lit with the help of a lantern. Aftab stumbled over a hole in the mud floor. At the far end, on a raised platform, a little bird-like boy sat behind a wooden desk. The boy, however, was not a boy but an old man with most of his hair already white. He looked up at us with enthusiasm; we might have been his first customers of the evening.

Holding her hand, the little old man inquired from Anuradha her date of birth. Without letting go of her, as though he feared she might fly away, he consulted a voluminous book. When he turned once again to her I was struck by little beads of perspiration on his brow. I thought he looked disturbed. Aftab shifted his weight from one foot to the other. He, too, perhaps had sensed the astrologer's discomfort.

Next door, the dance heated up, the tablas thumping away, the sarangi keeping a dutiful wail to another melancholy song of a woman's wait for her lover. (Could it be Krishna again?) The old man's prophecies, if such they were, were drowned out by the music and the clap of the dancer's feet. Anuradha's consultations were abruptly over. She pulled away her hand, opened her bag and handed the old man his fees. He looked at us, expectant but unsure. He could not have been in the business too long, to judge by his diffidence. I did not believe in astrology but, on an impulse, I took Anuradha's place on the platform.

'Please think of a flower,' the old man stammered out.

I thought of the marigolds in Azizun's balcony.

'Marigolds?' said the astrologer tentatively.

'Absolutely!' I laughed.

This triumph raised his spirits a bit. We waited, like boxers in a ring, wondering who was to call the next shot.

'There is something that I want,' I began.

'Yes.'

'Will I get it?'

He stared at my palm for a minute.

'Can you tell me what it is that you want?' His diffidence had returned.

The idea of the shares crossed my mind.

'I cannot tell you that,' I said.

After another minute of palm-staring, he said, 'It is a girl friend that you want.'

'A girl friend?'

'A *premika*.'

'Possibly.'

'You will not get her,' he said gruffly, as though getting something unpleasant off his chest.

I stared at him in silence. The dance next door had come to an end. All of a sudden it was very quiet. I dared not speak in the silence. The astrologer's glance hopped from me to the other two and back. He sighed as if he had understood something. In a minute, his understanding changed into agitation.

'No... No...,' he cried incoherently. 'No... No.'

He wrote something on a paper and handed it to me: 'You should do this *mantra jap* one lakh times.'

The interview had ended on the usual silly note. I gave him his fees. Aftab was next. His was the longest session, although it seemed more like a polite argument carried on among experts. From time to time, Aftab looked back at us and smiled, his goggles reflecting the dull lantern. The astrologer was certainly much more at ease with him than he had been with us. I wondered if he had realized that he was talking to people who were enemies of each other, appearances to the contrary.

Finally, the arguments ended and we stepped out into the open. We looked at each other wondering, perhaps, what each of us had separately been told.

We halted near a row of sweet shops. A thin reedy music now blared out of a gramophone, the records running higher than the prescribed r.p.m.'s Against its noise, conversation was impossible. What would have happened in that noise to the juggler's drums or the old man's song? Aftab and Anuradha had kulfis. I ordered a cup of tea. I envied them their habits. No doubt they always had kulfis whenever they went out. What did Anuradha and I have in common? Several like me had, perhaps, walked through her life. Even now she probably had lovers (where did she disappear for hours) who had greater claims on her than I ever had. The thought of the juggler crossed my mind. I was filled with self-pity and bitterness. Looking at her ravaged face, so intent on the kulfi in the plastic plate, I wondered what, after all, did I know of her. What had she shared with me besides a few of her goofy ideas and that bit of khir? In the dazzling glare, the pits in her face stood out. How many passers-by would have found her irresistible the way I did. Sitting in Bombay, I had imagined I had gotten over her but the last few hours had turned everything upside down. I was as much in love with this pock-marked phantom as ever.

~

Aftab's haveli lay in darkness. The car lights threw gigantic shadows of the fountain on the wall behind. Getting off the car, exhausted, I stepped off in the dead grass and reeled, cursing myself for not being able to control myself. We walked into the Blue Room but I did not stay there. I went quickly up to my room. I had a bad headache. I lay down without undressing and, drugged by the monotonous whirl of the fan, fell asleep.

I dreamt I was in a narrow alley at the end of which a shroud lay. Tall houses stood on both sides of the alley. They were purple in the moonlight with black gashes for windows. The alley and the houses were deserted. I knew who was under the shroud but could not recall his name. Then, the alley turned into the Blue Room with Aftab's ancestors smiling down at me. Azizun was singing. I heard her clearly although I could not see her. The power went off. The fan came to a standstill. I dreamt I dried my brow on the sleeve of my shirt. Then there was another hand, holding a handkerchief mopping my brow. I sat up.

'You!'

'I heard you groaning in your sleep.'

'Is Aftab asleep?'

'Sort of. And what have you been doing?'

'I have been dreaming and listening.'

'To what?'

'To myself.'

'And what have you heard?'

'I have heard,' I said steadying myself, 'I have heard that I should kill myself.'

Anuradha fiddled with the buttons on my shirt. 'You don't know what you are saying.'

I let her think that. Because the thought was dreadful. I did not know I was going to say that until I had said it. When I had said it though, I knew it was true. That was why I was horrified.

'And I have heard other things.'

'What things?'

'I heard a great threshing of the wind way up in the sky. And it says, I want. I want.'

'What do you want?'

And while I tried to forge a reply to fool her, to laugh the whole thing off, a sob arose from somewhere choking me off. In the darkness, tears flowed down my cheeks, into the pillow. Anuradha peered into my face. I could see the whites of her eyes. 'What's wrong?' she whispered, her hands tightening on my shoulders.

I wanted to choke the flow, grab the valve that controlled them. The tears flowed on, silent, independent of me. I looked around in despair. 'Why should this have happened to me in this strange room, so far from home?' I said.

'But this, too, is your home.'

I patted her cheek. 'You are very nice. Maybe it is you I want.'

'You don't want me. You don't know what you want. You don't know what is wrong and you don't know what you want.'

The coloured ventilators blurred, focussed again.

'Have you got any cigarettes? The usual stuff, not those fancy once. I have run out of mine.'

'I can get some.'

She went out and returned with a packet.

She lighted a cigarette and handed it to me. It tasted of her lipstick. She lit another for herself. I felt better.

'I know what is wrong,' I said.

Anuradha nodded. She sat very close to me but did not touch me. Yet I had the impression she was as much in need of physical contact as I.

'I'll tell you what is wrong,' I repeated trying to organize my thoughts. 'I am dislocated. My mind is out of focus. There is something sitting right in front of me and I cannot see it. Why am I here? Why *do* I come here? Because I want you. Why else?'

'But you come here for those shares. If it were me you wanted you wouldn't be going around buying up all those shares.'

'Are you bargaining with me?' I said.

'Not in the way *you* think I am bargaining.'

'What if I decide to stop buying those shares? Will you believe me, then?'

'You probably think Aftab sent me to achieve just this kind of exchange.'

'I don't know what I think. I can barely think in this house, in this room.'

'I know. I know. But I believe you. I don't mind what you think.'

~

She was tall, long-limbed, full. Not petite like Geeta. Or skinny like Leela Sabnis. There were scars on her belly, her breasts, scars that I could feel but not see. The coloured light, fusing over our bodies lent them a fourth dimension, as though we coupled high above the earth, independent of time and space, like a pair of asteroids, locked in each other's gravity. Silent, unable to communicate except what we communicated through the trust and push and pull of our bodies, we circled high above the empty cities. Or, perhaps, the silence, as usual, was only on my side, I never felt more alone than when locked in this, the most intimate of dialogues. I knew that. Others — Geeta, Leela — had perhaps sensed the aloneness and had left it undisturbed for fear of disturbing more than they could handle. Anuradha, on the other hand, was the daughter of disturbance itself. I could feel her pushing against this shroud of silence — with her hips, her mouth, her nails, her teeth and, finally, a prolonged, wild, hoarse crying that could have been the cry of the world's first lost lover, or of all men, destined as they are to cry, unfulfilled, to the stars.

9

The nights get cooler. The brief winter of Bombay has set in but my sleep is no better. At times, quite against K's orders, tired and defeated — by insomnia, by this chronicle — I walk about the beach on dark nights. 'When the sun is set and the moon is also set, and the fire has sunk down, and the voice is silent, what, then, Yajnavalkya, is the light of man?' What, indeed? These little tit bits buzz inside my head along with film tunes, slogans, Mr. Thapar's jingles for selling buckets. Now and then, they slip out of their prisons and mock me. What indeed did Yajnavalkya say? I sit on the little mound under the glacial shower of stars, thinking, mostly of her. I thought I had flushed her out of my system that night, ejaculated my obsession of her along with my seed. I had done that before with other women. I was certain I would never go back to her or to the morass of Aftab's haveli.

It looked ridiculous from the skyscrapers of Bombay: a tawdry, sensual den, a dead house in a dead city. Aftab's dargahs and temples were no less ridiculous for all their claims of commanding a mysterious world, as pretentious and meaningless as the holy bulls of Benaras. If there was nothing new under the sun, as he said, there was nothing new in them either, or in Lal Haveli, or in that room of Gargi's where, in a waking dream, I had once been. If there was nothing new under the sun, then whatever it was that I wanted, I was not going to get.

But I was just not myself. That was where the rub lay. I spent hours — in the office, at home, amidst the din of parties — struggling with her memory, trying to untie the riddle. With no effect. I must have had a great air of preoccupation those days; I could see it reflected in people's eyes. Mr. Thapar would be sitting across me, his grey hair neatly parted, watching me with a puzzled, speculative eye and I would not have a clue of what he had been saying and I would say, 'I am sorry. Could you please repeat that?' I had seen that gaze of Mr. Thapar's before, although I could not say where until one night, many months later, I remembered that that was how, towards the end, I had seen him observe my father.

'What do you know of sorrow?' Aftab had said amidst the burning *ghats* of the Manikarnika. How wrong could he be. I had sorrows that did not let me breathe. If I stayed up all night choffing tranquillizers, not knowing why I was awake, and came close to tears because I did not know, it came pretty close to sorrow. I had failed to make Geeta happy, or be anything more than a stranger to my children. My friends thought me a nut. I had been neglecting my companies. I had not even got over my mother's death. Or my father's, or the oppressive turbulence of the voids that never let me alone. Then, there was the greatest sorrow of them all — that no one even guessed: There was the sorrow of idleness. I had this idleness to cope with that no one knew of, not even Geeta or Mr. Thapar. It wasn't that I had time on my hands or that I sat about. Quite the contrary. I ran about all day and most of the night: wheeling, dealing, quarrelling. But there was always this bit of me, a large bit, somewhere between the head and the chest, just idling about like a stationary engine, getting involved with nothing. It made me feel as though I was asleep. This was no joke. In fact it was one of the weirdest things to happen to anybody. I would be sitting in a meeting, listening, making notes, even talking myself and the feeling would begin to seep into me that in fact I was asleep. Had it always been like that? Had I always been half asleep? Or, could it be that I once had a stable, wakeful life but had gradually lost my bearings? My good friend Leela Sabnis said one was fully programmed by the time one was five. So, I must have been like that — half asleep, half awake — all this time.

Maybe, it was this sleep that I had first to break. If I knew what had put me to sleep I could, perhaps, get rid of it like one got rid of a hangover. That night, in Gargi's room, I thought a shadow had brushed past me, touching me lightly, telling me how to rouse myself but then all was confusion once again.

Everything was a haze. Time itself seemed wiped off like the spools of a computer. The first casualty was sleep which had always been fragile. I had long spells of insomnia which left me drained and depressed the following day. It was during one such low that, walking down the aisles of a book store, I ran into Leela Sabnis.

'My God, Som, how you have changed!' was the first thing she said.

'For the better, I hope.'

Leaning against the stacks, she looked me up and down, her light eyes bright as ever.

'You are looking older than your age, you know.' Leela was never one to hide her thoughts.

'You are as young as ever,' I said. 'Teaching still?'

'No, I am in advertising now.'

'Well, well, you never know!'

She put her hand on my arm. 'Come to my digs. They aren't far.'

She had bought a tiny flat with the money her father left her. He had died since we last met. Sitting on the floor, back against a wall, feet up on a chair, I wondered how she felt with her father gone.

'You were quite attached to him, weren't you?' I addressed her in the little kitchen where she stirred the coffee.

'I guess I was.'

'Is that why you left teaching?'

'Could be. Anyway, I want to leave psychology alone, like. For a while, at least.'

Leela was several years younger to me but, at times, she put on mannerisms that belonged to an even younger generation. But I was fond of her. She was, in a way, the only surviving landmark of a past that, although ten years old, seemed to have existed ages ago. It might have been in another birth. How I had chased to get her into bed. That, I believed, then, was all I wanted. As she came out of the kitchen carrying the coffee mugs, I searched her face for clues that might reveal why I had so pursued her ten years earlier. She was a fine looking person with regular features and nice eyes. She wore jeans and a man's white shirt. Her hair was browner than before and cut like a man's. She had that peculiar neatness and straight carriage that young working girls have these days. Like the secretaries in our office. She had intelligence in her face and conversation. She was a fine product of Bombay, of India. As she squatted down, her feet raised on the platform shoes, I noticed her fair ankles. I was reminded of Azizun's finely turned instep and how she played with her *pajeb* when she was idle.

We settled down with coffees, lit cigarettes.

'Busy as ever?' she asked.

'Sort of.'

'I hear a lot about you, how fast you have been growing. The rumour is you are buying up a lot of companies.'

'Most of them would close down anyway,' I said, trying to cover up my indifference. But it was hard to cover up things from Leela Sabnis. From above the rim of her cup she looked at me quizzically as though looking at a new man.

'What's the matter? You have lost enthusiasm?'

'I don't know.'

On an impulse Leela leaned forward, ruffled my hair and laughed. 'You still hear that music, air threshed way up in the sky, I want... I want, or some such thing. It used to be quite a record.'

I laughed, relieved at being made fun of.

'I still hear that particular record, I am afraid, much as I would like to shut it off.'

'It is a problem of identity, I suppose.'

'I didn't think problems of identity existed for people of my age.'

'You would be surprised. There are people whose sense of identity at the end of life doesn't go beyond: I own this house; earn so much; have four children; drive this car; have so much in the bank and so on. Maybe such identity is not enough for you.'

'I don't see why not.'

'I suppose you can't take your identity from your caste.'

'What caste?'

'You are a brahmin, after all.'

'A Bhaskar, what is a Bhaskar doing in business?'

A pain, as physical as of a wound, shot through me every time I thought of Anuradha or heard her name. Leela said: 'Or, may be the identity of an extended joint family.'

I kept quiet, sipping coffee, thinking vaguely of other ill-defined things. Leela meant well but she was always seeking explanations, immediately, fiercely. She could be a pain in the neck.

We went on like this for another half hour. 'Or, maybe,' she was saying, 'maybe what you want is a mystical identification, identification with a godhead, as most Hindus want, sooner or later.'

'I want no such thing.'

'You haven't got the stamina for that, I know. You haven't got the faith. You have always been a sceptic. You always will be.'

That was enough of explanation for one morning. I said, 'You are damn right. Now come and have lunch with me.'

We went to a mod-mod cafe on the top floor of a wondrous new hotel. It was a monument of marble and shining glass. On tables of Mysore teak, bright yellow spreads lay along with polished cutlery. There was a bar and we had several martinis before getting around to lunch. Wine was poured for us in crystal goblets. The place was full of foreign tourists. They stood by the massive windows and admired the view of the harbour. Vikrant, the aircraft carrier, lay at anchor as it had, the day my father and I went to the Elephanta Caves.

The steward, handsome in his dark blue jacket, greeted us. 'Seeing you after a long time, sir. Have you been out of station?'

'Yes,' I said. In a way, Aftab's haveli was another station, another world. There was laughter and the tinkle of glass and the soft murmur of foreign tongues. I felt the miasma of Lal Haveli lifting, dissolving before the vitality of this throbbing cosmopolitan life. Benaras, Aftab, Anuradha, their haveli — all were bores, frogs stuck in their ancient marshy wells. What I wanted, I decided, was to go abroad, get the hell away from this land of obsessions.

So I took off with Geeta for Europe and America, presumably for business. Nothing was more welcome just then than the roar of wide-bodied jets, the sleepless, burning universe of airports that griddled the world. The vision of men, who had designed the jets and laid out the airports, had an authority that could not be matched by the designers of Aftab's labyrinth. New York, with its monuments of concrete and aluminium and its svelte women, their thighs rosy and slim under the mini-skirts, its dazzling bazaars and a face that had no past, was the haven that I needed. It contained, at the very least, a promise that I recognized. Geeta reeled under the fury of our travels. It had been years since she had been out with me like that. There were new lines about her face, and her body had lost some of its firmness but she had a charm all her own as well as that trust which did not waver as I stripped her before large mirrors in silent hotel rooms while thirty storeys below the traffic of Europe and America and Japan hurtled by. Or, did, at times, a pensive light pass through those soft eyes? Was there on her lips an unframed question that I was too drunk to notice? Was she puzzled by lust followed so startlingly by impotence? She must have, at times, wondered if it was just the whisky, as I always claimed before passing out. Then, one night, in Tokyo, on the last leg of our travels, semi-awake from a dream, I found her under me, her breath hot against my cheek, her eyes staring up into mine, restless with desire, then frustrated but comprehending, as I rolled off her, the blood draining out of me as swiftly as consciousness crept in. Geeta cried then, quietly, as was her wont, her little hands knotted in fists straight by her side. Petrified by my own sudden knowledge, I could do little beyond uttering incoherent noises. I lay awake a long time after she went to sleep. I could see it all: the room with ventilators of stained glass, the peacock on the carpet, the dark red floor. And Anuradha on the bed naked, gasping, her dark triangle almost touching my cheek. I drugged myself back to sleep, shuddering an hour later into a tormented wakefulness. I stood by a window and gazed at Tokyo through a blind. The skyscrapers grew out of the rock, like pins on a cushion. A grey, watery dawn broke in the east, the smog soaking up the light like a blotter soaks up ink. The struggle went on in the sky while on the ground Tokyo roused and threw itself into work. I decided we had to return by the first available flight.

Returning to Bombay, at four in the morning, walking towards the glass exits, I slipped on the polished floor. I lay perspiring for an hour in the car and at the house, my head in Geeta's lap. 'It is the exhaustion of the travel,' everyone said, everyone except K. He monitored the cardiograms without a word. I heard Geeta quiz him outside the door. 'He will be all right. Don't worry.' And all right I soon was except that I couldn't leave the bed. I felt as though struck by thunder, bled totally of all energy. Inside me, there was nothing but an empty roaring, like the roar of the sea in a conch. It slowly dawned upon me that I enjoyed staying in bed. I kept the discovery to myself lest it should start a new chain of enquiries. But K, too, suspected it and came along one evening when Geeta was not home. He sat about, smoking, listening to the records that I had brought back from the trip. Finally, he said, 'You know, Som, there was nothing wrong with any of those ECG's I took.'

'What do you mean?'

'What I mean is that there is nothing as such wrong with you.'

'What is "as such"?'

'What I want to know is are you hamming it?'

I laughed. 'I wish I were. But this is not my kind of hamming, you know.'

'One never knows what is one's brand. Your father was not above hamming himself. He did a lot of it towards the end without realizing what he was doing.'

He looked at me through his cool steady eyes. 'If you know what I mean,' he added after a pause. He did not elaborate but I got his meaning and was shattered by the understanding. I certainly didn't want melancholia if that was what he had in mind.

'Very well,' I said. 'I shall get up tomorrow and I shall go to the office.'

'Is that really what you want to do?'

'I don't know what I want to do.'

He kept quiet.

10

When I went back, it was to Gargi. With the rains the heat had declined. A damp musty wind blew along the *ghats*. It had long since blown out the rickshaw puller's lamp but we were still far from the heavy traffic and the policemen. He had finished his peddling of fine young ladies who sang and did excellent *chikan* work and could be induced to do other things. He was breathless now, his lungs wrecked by ten years of smoking and rickshaw pulling. As we passed under the street lamps, I noticed the steady increase in the perspiration down his back. His muscles twitched in jerky movements, as though they existed independent of him.

That morning I had had breakfast in Bombay. To Geeta I had said I was going to Delhi on business which was not a lie because I might have done just that and gone back. I had no clear idea what I planned to do in Benaras. K had suggested I stop hamming. How did I know where all I would wander before the hamming stopped, *if* it stopped at all.

The light of the *chowk* approached, trembling through a haze of dust. The rickshaw man got off, lighted the lamp, cleared his lungs of phlegm. 'I can take you to little children,' he said desperately, as though offering me the accumulated innocence of Benaras' children.

'Take me to the cinema hall with mirror doors.'

That was all that I remembered of the location.

It was just then that I had decided to go to Gargi. I felt at home with her. I wanted to talk, to explain, to understand. I remembered Aftab's plaintive peevish complaints to her, and the thought crossing my mind: 'She understands. The only one who understands.'

I sat across from Gargi. The windows had been flung open letting in the noise and the smell of the streets. Gargi sat in her usual place, against the wall, straight-backed, watching me through pleasant, intelligent eyes. She was not surprised to see me. I might as well have dropped in from the house next door.

I had a cough. There was a dryness in my nose and my throat. She got up — how neat and cool she looked — and got me a glass of water in a steel tumbler. She watched me drink it down, then opened her paan box. She made up a paan, offered it to me. I remembered refusing it during the first visit. I took it now. I thought I needed it. She made another for herself. She sat back, her hands clasped around her knees, and smiled at me through stained teeth. Once again, I wanted to hug her.

'You know, I have been away.' She watched my lips, nodded.

'After I met you the last time I went abroad. To Europe and America and Japan. With Geeta, my wife. I would like her to meet you some time. She is your type. Believes in God. Krishna and all that.' Gargi smiled.

'I have not been well. Bombay is still quite warm. The heat has been getting me down. It was nice and cool everywhere we went. Now, we are back in this blasted heat. You are wondering why I am in Benaras? The fact is I don't know. I didn't know I would be coming to Benaras when I left Bombay this morning. Maybe, I wanted to see you. I am staying at the hotel. We took nearly an hour getting here.'

An interval passed in silence.

'I am fed up of this restlessness,' I shot out suddenly. 'So absolutely fed up. Can you help me?' I had tried to make a jest of it but my voice trembled. Gargi looked at me closely, scrutinized my face. I don't think she had heard me.

'Can you help me?' I said again. As I watched, her expression changed. She had been deeply touched. She took out her pad.

'God will send someone to help you.'

'Who?'

She smiled, wrote again, 'Someone who has known suffering.'

'But what if there is no God?'

Gargi quietly tucked the pad under the mat, nodded, smiled.

Across the street, a ramshackle temple, a favourite of the prostitutes, came alive with the evening *aarati.* 'Prayer does not change God,' Kierkegaard had said, 'but it changes him who prays.' Maybe, I ought to start attending temples every evening.

Gargi got up, entered the little kitchen. She took down a brass thali and started to lay out the food which the girl must have left. There was rice and curds and a mysterious vegetable. I realized I was hungry. I ate in silence. She watched me eat. I said, 'How is everyone? Azizun?' She did not catch me so I repeated the question. She nodded slowly.

'You know, those little girls — the ones Azizun teaches — they really work hard at their dancing. I watched them the last time. Azizun still lives downstairs? And Aftab? Have you seen him lately?' I didn't know why I was prattling on unless I was trying to build some bridge to Aftab's world. It was getting late but I had no desire to leave. I could have slept right there if Gargi had permitted. The noises of the street had been gradually dying out. It was cooler. Gargi opened her paan box again and made paans for both of us. Then she wrote out a note for me. 'Aftab is not well. I am going to see him. Come with me.' I looked at her uncertainly. She nodded, smiled. There was the sound of the front door opening, followed by Tarakki's heavy step. Mouth full of paan juice and lips red, I stared at him. Gargi closed her *paandaan,* picked up her cane — I never understood why she carried that cane around — and got ready to go. I was wondering what to do with myself when she bent down, caught me by the wrist, tugged me along down the stairs where the car waited.

~

Aftab, goggles and all, against the head board of the bed. I had never been to his room or, to that part of the haveli. It was far removed from the Blue Room and the room in which I used to stay. The single bed was covered with a green sheet. There was a spittoon. His chess board stood on a side-table. It was a narrow room with ventilators next to the high ceiling. It did not look as though

Anuradha shared this room. Azizun, who had been waiting on him, now came forward to greet Gargi.

Aftab looked gaunt, yellow. Perspiration poured down his face. He wore narrow pyjamas and a kurta of very fine *mul.* He reminded me of a portrait of Bahadur Shah. He took no notice of my presence.

I wondered what the matter was with him. Gargi sat by his side, her hand on his forehead. He talked hoarsely to her. I could not catch what he said. Neither could have Anuradha who stood equally removed. From her expression, she might have been as much of a stranger as myself. Gargi patted Aftab's hand, a picture of motherly good humour.

The scene had the quality of tableau that had been staged many times before. Whenever, I imagined, Aftab's precariously balanced nerves received a shock. Each actor knew his appointed role, including, perhaps, Aftab. At one point, he lifted his goggles, dabbed his eyes with a handkerchief, then carried on rapidly. He improved, gained energy, as he talked to Gargi. His words, although still hoarse, came out more clearly. He did not perspire as profusely. Gargi encouraged him to go on. She wanted him, perhaps, to get things off his chest, talk himself into sleep. Presently, signs of exhaustion appeared. His back lost the iron-like rigidity. His voice became feebler.

It was only now that I became aware of the tension in the room. A ritual it might have been but it was obviously a tense one: For both Azizun and Anuradha and, strangely, even for me. What meaning could it possibly have held for me, a stranger, so unexpectedly present? I shook my head in disbelief. I wondered what precise shock Aftab had received this time. Why did I feel guilty? The tension had begun to blow away though. Anuradha, dressed as ever in her dated costumes, was visibly relaxed. So was Azizun. In a little while, Aftab fell silent, slid under the green counter-pane and fell asleep.

Azizun stayed with Aftab. Anuradha and I followed Gargi down a couple of stairs into another room. It might have been a replica of Gargi's room in the bazaar. There was a mat, a pitcher of water, some books. A Sri Chakra, drawn on parchment and framed, hung on one wall. It looked like a piece of rare art and a decoration rather than anything else. It might have come down in the collections of Aftab's ancestors. We sat on the mats. Gargi did not look any worse for her exercise with Aftab. What with the heat and talk and the travel of the day, I felt very tired. Gargi noticed it and, patted my arm.

'Why don't you go to sleep?' Anuradha said to me.

'I think I will.'

'I will take you to your room.'

'I will go back to the hotel.'

'At this time of the night!'

'Tarakki will drop me. I can find a rickshaw.'

'You are being difficult,' Anuradha said with a sigh.

I was aware of a strident childish clamour in my voice. I had thought of Anuradha, lusted after her all these weeks, but now that we were face to face I was resisting her, fighting her off. I wanted her and at the same time resented my need for her. I also resented that she had somehow seen more of me than I would have liked to reveal. Faced with her, in the loneliness of that haveli, I realized how inadequate I was to deal with her. Even for this I blamed her. It was silly.

'I don't want to stay here,' I said, sulking.

Gargi had been watching me with amusement. She pulled out her slim little pad and passed me a note. 'Go with her,' it said. 'Don't quarrel. She is your *shakti.*' To this day, I do not know what Gargi meant by that. But Anuradha, I learnt that night, was indispensable to me.

~

I was fated to return to that haveli over and over. We possessed each other with singular ferocity, neither willing to loosen the clasp.

Yet each meeting, far from cooling my passions, served only to fuel them. I lived on the nourishment of the shades thrown by her naked body under the chromatic shower. Beyond that room lay the silent labyrinth through which, too, before the invisible audience of Aftab and Azizun and Tarakki, I sometimes walked. By myself or with Anuradha, hand in hand. And always in various shades of coherence, the spoken or unspoken question, like a vulture, circled the corpse of my life: what lay in the last labyrinth?

From these penumbral regions, at intervals, I returned to Bombay, picking up the threads which, in any event, were carried very well by Mr. Thapar. If he suspected things he made no mention of them, nor did he inquire about our suspension of purchases of Aftab's shares. In Bombay, invigorated by tall buildings and swift lifts, a bracing give and take of commerce, I would soon be my old self and wonder if Aftab's Haveli was not a horror-dream, drummed up by a sick imagination. It would seem, indeed, that I must be equally sick to return to it. But, then, turning on a golden hinge — a fragrance, a tapestry, the sound of a dripping tap — the swing of the pendulum would begin and very soon I would be back in the little room with the stained glass ventilators and a peacock on the rug and the embrace of a strange woman whose distance from me, for all the loving, seemed never to diminish.

Once, in the middle of a warm night, I heard the sound of drums and hoarse happy voices singing. I sat up, untying the knots of our naked limbs, feeling for a moment lost, as though in a different, if not unfamiliar, country. A song came floating on the air, indistinct but haunting, like the song of the old man at the carnival.

'My mother used to sing that song,' Anuradha said.

I looked at her. What did I know of her except that I could not live without her?

'You were born in Bombay?' I asked.

'Mr. Thapar should know.'

'Don't be ridiculous. Tell me.'

'In Biharsharif. You know where it is?'

I nodded.

'In a house with one room where in the evening my mother sang for strangers.' She paused. 'You want to know more?'

She lit one of Aftab's cigarettes, a sign, I knew by now, of tension and distress. I put my arm around her naked waist.

'I have to know,' I said. She smiled.

'Later in the evening someone would stay on. Then a man came and refused to leave. He was tall and very thin. He had a black beard and large black eyes. He carried a suitcase full of bank notes which he gave to my mother. He drank. A week after he moved in with us, he went out and returned with a crate of bottles. The bottles rattled as he dragged them from one end of the room to the other. He drank every evening. He sat drinking and stared unblinking at mother while she sang. There were mangroves in Biharsharif. Sometimes, on summer evenings, we took walks. One day we moved to Gwalior. We had a bungalow at the edge of the town. Now, my mother also drank. At times they quarrelled at night when it was very quiet. The bungalow shook with the sound of their shouting. I would lie in bed and feel as though a storm raged outside. I would start to tremble and the trembling would go on for hours. It was a disease, I knew, but I dared not tell anyone. In the morning, holding each other, they cried, the man and my mother. My mother sat before Krishna and sang and wept. Then, one night, the shouting suddenly ceased. The man stabbed her twelve times with a broken whisky bottle and hung himself from a hook which was meant for a fan.'

'Good God, Anuradha,' I stammered out.

'My name was Meera, then.'

She fell silent. Outside, on the quiet air, the song flowed on. I put my hand on her shoulder. She laid her cheek on it. Her warm tears flowed silently across the back of my hand.

'It must have been terrible.'

'I don't remember. I was only a child. My aunt brought me to Bombay, put a uniform on me, changed my name, and sent me to a convent.'

'After all you have been through...' I began.

'It is nothing. In that world it is nothing, not even a drop.'

'Still... How do you manage to live with it?'

'Like others have done before me.'

'And how did they do it?'

'I don't know.'

Suddenly, she turned towards me and took hold of my wrists. 'I wish we had never met. I wish you had not come to Aftab's party. I wish you had never come to this haveli.'

'Let us go away from here.'

'Go where?'

'Come to Bombay.'

She laughed. 'I can't do that.'

'Why not?'

'You won't understand. But I like to live here. With Aftab, Gargi.'

I started to speak. She put a hand on my lips and pulled me down to her breasts.

'Don't talk,' she whispered against my ear. 'Don't talk.' Her voice trailed off. The distance remained.

And so to diminish the distance, to grab her, to possess her wholly, I hustled her off to the hills, to a beautiful valley in the shadow of snow-covered peaks. There, I thought, no one would know her and she would think of none and there would be no one to distract her from her loving of me. What she said to Aftab, I did not know. Or, perhaps, he did not care, busy as he seemed in preparing for his annual trip to Lucknow.

In the mountains, through the mist and the rain and the sprinkling of sunny days, I clung to her. I threw myself, my entire desperate weight, the turbulence of my forty years, on her.

How did she bear the sheer ferocity of it all!

She was made for the hills. She laughed at little things, talked a lot. I discovered the fineness of her Urdu. But her Urdu also brought, gliding into the firelit evenings, the ghost of Aftab, until one evening I had to ask, 'Did he teach you?'

'Yes.' After a pause she added, 'Is he still your rival?'

'What do you mean?'

'Are you still fighting with him, if not for his company for... for something else that is...?'

'That is his?' I finished the sentence for her.

'Yes.'

'But are you his?'

'Am I not?'

'You don't sound certain.'

'I am not certain.'

That did not set me at rest. If she was not Aftab's nor, perhaps, was she mine. To lift my spirits, I drank.

Then one evening, when I began my drinking she said she too would drink. It was the first time she had asked for a drink since that evening at the Intercontinental. I was surprised, happy. Buoyed up with whisky, when I moved alone across moonless skies, I had never been sure where she stood. Curled up on the frayed velvet arm chair, her eyes fixed on me, she had bothered me at times. I was glad, therefore, that she too was coming where I went every cold evening.

She drank easily with just that extra swiftness that marks out the novice. She held to me the empty glass, the fire and the alcohol suffusing her face with a new glow. She stared at me, her eyes black, unfathomable, shining in the firelight.

When was it, how many drinks later, when I imagined myself at last aloft from the dark planet, when was it that, naked, she walked unsteadily to a window, peered into the darkness, tapped the glass panes as though she knocked at a door. I followed her, wanting desperately the warmth of her body. I stood beside her, my palm against her belly. In a voice flat and ambiguous, she said, 'There is a god up there.'

'Up where?'

'In those mountains.'

There were the mountains all right, a purple mass, as they might have been the night of the first volcanic upheaval that gave them birth. And, there, high above them, were the snow-covered peaks, glowing in the light of the moon.

'How do you know?' I said.

'I know.'

'Rubbish.' I said.

'There is a temple there. On a hill lined with lepers. You must come with me.'

'I am not a leper.'

'I did not mean that. But you must come. God will cure you.'

'Cure me of what? A bad heart? Fears? Disappointments?'

She said she could not explain. I looked into her drunken eyes and, in a way, I understood. Deep inside my heart I knew I was a leper, that I needed a cure. But I refused to yield ground.

'You are absurd,' I told her.

And while I was telling her how absurd she was, she fell into my arms, trembling and very cold.

I picked her up — I had the strength, then — and carried her to the bed near the fire. She lay still, inert, her head in my lap, shivering every few seconds. In my unquenchable hunger I made love to her. It was like making love to a corpse. She just wasn't there. Later, I sat by her slumbering body and, unaccountably, wept.

I lay awake angry with myself, angrier still at her dragging God into that room which until that moment had been the stage for satisfying my wildest fantasies. A mountain wind howled around the Guest House. As I sank into sleep its howl turned into the tired ancient cry: I want. I want. I want.

All of the next day we wandered in the bright sunlight. I searched her face for traces of the god that had so possessed her the previous night. There was none. All she said was: 'Did I pass out?' 'You did,' I said, my voice hoarse with tenderness. To counter this shadow that had so unexpectedly fallen between us, I took her up a hillside, into a copse of pines, and made love to her. 'Not here,' she cried in awe, blushing, but she liked it and it was only when I saw her loving it, stretching her body to the limits of pleasure, surrendering to the moment, that I, at last, felt reassured.

We sat on the verandah of the Guest House. The setting sun dropped between two trees, a ball of orange fire. We watched it sink. The air became chilly. The last rays focused for a moment on Anuradha's face making her irises glow. With the light gone, I felt the return of the phantom of the previous night. He was palpable, whoever it was that had joined us on the darkening verandah. Anuradha was aware of him, too, but pretended otherwise. She laughed unnecessarily, called for tea although we had just had some. She made fun of the honeymooning couple who stayed next door.

'If I got married I could never have worn red bangles like those.'

'Aftab talks as though he did marry you.'

'He lives in a dream world. Anyway, what difference does it make?'

'Wouldn't you like to be married to someone?'

'I can imagine I am married to Aftab. I can imagine I am married to you. My mother used to imagine she was married to Krishna.'

I squirmed at the mention of the word.

'Whenever that man in Gwalior asked her to marry her she told him she was married to Krishna.'

'So he killed her.'

'Probably.'

The laughter, even a pretension of it, was gone. I could see her sinking rapidly down the abyss.

‘I wish it would never grow dark,’ she said.

That night she drank again. She drank with a new intensity but in silence. She did not even talk of God, which, perversely, disappointed me. For some reason, as I rose higher, it was about God that I wanted to hear. But Anuradha did not talk, did not explain. When she spoke at last, she tottered on the brink of hysteria. She wept and struggled to keep her weeping down. When I tried to touch her she moved away, her tear drenched face reflecting emotions that I did not understand. She went to her bed and, presently, fell into a drunken stupor. In the morning she said, ‘Som, I want to go back.’

11

I addressed Gargi: ‘There is a lizard, Hatteria, on the islands of New Zealand, that has a third eye, just like Shiva's. The other reptiles of its class went extinct at the end of the Jurassic, about a hundred million years ago.’

This was the sort of odds and ends that at one time I was a master of: the circumference of the earth; temperatures of Terra del Fuego, the structure of the DNA, electron shells, atomic weights, computer circuits. Nothing had interested me more than the secrets of the universe. Blessed little good all that curiosity had done me.

I did not know what had triggered me off. We sat in Gargi's house. It had been raining when I arrived from the airport. They were waiting for me in the Blue Room, Aftab and Azizun. Anuradha walked in a little later. I could hear that rustle of her sari before she appeared. She was dressed as if for a wedding.

‘It is Janmashtami,’ Aftab said, as though it explained all. ‘Let's go.’ To me it explained nothing, but I went.

At the temple a minor stampede separated us. Alone, I sat smoking on a marble slab under a concrete awning. Crowds streamed past me and across the rain-soaked yard of the temple. It was still raining. The slab I sat on was meant to be fixed on the floor but had not yet been fixed. It tilted every time I leaned a little too far. Some time back a band of dancing bhaktas had rammed into my sector of the crowd, separating me from the rest. There were lights everywhere. Also shadows. My slab was in shadow. I had rolled up my trousers. My feet were bare and wet. Sitting there, I smoked and peeled my toe nails.

From the corner of my eye, I saw Anuradha hurrying by. I called out to her. She came running through the puddles holding her sari off the ground. Her face was flushed.

'I have been looking for you all over.'

'Well, here I am.'

'Come on, then. There isn't much time.'

'For what? For the Lord to be born?'

'Oh, you! Aren't you coming?'

I thought of her standing naked near a window saying, 'There is a god in that mountain.'

'I am not coming,' I said.

'Please.'

'Too crowded for my taste.'

'I'll go then.'

'I'll wait here.'

She went off, her figure marvellous in the shadows. I felt frustrated, jealous. Of whom, I did not know. She had said another thing that first night standing by the window. She had wanted me to visit the god, walk up a steep mountain road and pay my respects.

'Rubbish,' I had said.

Finally, an unbelievable tumult engulfed the temple. Conches were blown, bells struck. A chant arose from the multitude which might as likely have been a wail. The god had once again been born.

And, now, we were back in Gargi's house. It was nearly dawn. I felt better, encouraged by Gargi's presence.

'So, there is this lizard with a third eye,' I looked around. Anuradha smiled. She somehow seemed drunk to me. Aftab stared back, impassive.

'Are you awake?'

'Yes,' he said, I returned to Gargi.

'So, the earth burning, whirling in space, gradually cools down. The seas and the swamps appear. Great upheavals occur, on the top of mountains, in the beds of the seas. And all the time, the earth is whirling through space. Water plants and algae appear. The protozoans, the jawless fishes, the cartilage fishes. Four hundred million years ago fishes developed gills and lungs.'

'Are you listening?' I asked Gargi which was a stupid thing to say.

Gargi smiled, nodded.

'So the fishes develop gills and lungs. Fifty million years later some of them venture out on land. The amphibians arrive. It wasn't easy for them to survive. They had to fight gravity — and much else. But they did survive. There was mutation and selection again. The reptiles evolved. The earth began to be populated for the first time. The age of reptiles began, producing the snake, iguana, the dinosaur.

'After a hundred million years, selection developed another great improvement — the placenta. It was a revolutionary development. The mammals' future was guaranteed. Or, so at least, it seemed. The mammals led to the primates, to man himself. The brain grew; hands could clutch; eyes moved towards the front; vision became stereoscopic. Man gradually took his place.'

High on Aftab's hospitality, stirred by Gargi, I soared. 'And now, a totally new development takes place, something happens along an altogether different dimension. An animal shape is developed that can shelter the spirit, mind you, the Spirit, something that hadn't existed before. Revolution of quite unpredictable dimensions is on the way. You see my point?'

Gargi nodded.

'The Spirit was already there at the time of the Cro-magnons, more than forty thousand years ago. You can see it at Lascaux.'

'And of course,' I added, 'it is still there.'

My excitement fizzled out as quickly as it had erupted. I came crashing down from my starry heights. 'You see what bothers me is why this should have happened?'

'Why what should have happened?' said Aftab.

'Why should there be this turn to evolution? Why should Man be equipped, burdened, with this strange... this strange sensibility, or urge or drive? Is it by chance? Or, is there a meaning to it? Is it superstition? The moral influence of others? I have my doubts about all those explanations. Moreover, how did those *others* get the morals in the first place?'

'What is your explanation?' Aftab said.

'I don't have an explanation. But that does not matter. The point is that this Spirit is there. And if it is there, if Man has inherited it, then what is he to do with it? In other words, what precisely is expected of him, of you and me, of Anuradha, of everyone else? Darwin didn't say how we are supposed to evolve further.'

There was a long silence. Then, Aftab said, 'It is a matter of visions.'

'Visions?'

'There must be men and women who see what you want to see.'

I shrugged.

'You don't take me seriously,' he said sullenly, his attention beginning to wander.

'Oh, I take you seriously enough...,' I said, trying to pierce the curtain of his goggles. '... Except I don't think it is a matter of visions. Visions are dime a dozen.'

'Ha, I must explain to you one of these days,' said Aftab and got up. 'You are very headstrong, you know,' he added.

I kept quiet.

'I must go now,' he said, abruptly taking leave.

'When do we meet again?' he said from the door.

'I am leaving in the morning.'

'You come and go like the wind. That also is not good. Anyway, good luck to you.'

'Thanks,' I said.

After Aftab was gone Anuradha said, 'Maybe Krishna begins where Darwin left off.' Her remark surprised me. She was like the ocean; one could never reach the bottom of her. Her mother never told her about her father. For all I knew, he might have been a genius.

'I never thought of it like that,' I said.

'But what is Krishna?' I wanted to add. All of a sudden, though, I wasn't much interested in the argument, I wasn't interested in Darwin or Krishna, or the spirit of the Cro-magnons. All I wanted was her. I wanted her body and soul, every bit of her. I wasn't willing to share a hair of her body with anyone. She looked like I had never seen her before: draped in a sari of heavy silk, its muted colours woven on the loom of some exquisite ancient craftsman of Kanchi, she looked like a medieval courtesan around whom wars might have been fought. There was a diamond in her nose which had not been there before. She sat against the wall, chin on her drawn knees, dainty feet together, watching me. There was *mehndi* on her hands. All this preparation, I knew, was for Krishna, but I could make believe it was for me. She straightened suddenly as though in a spasm. Her sari slipped from her shoulder revealing one full breast. For an insane moment I thought I could feel between my knees the firm flesh of her thighs. We stared at each other, consumed by our hunger, oblivious of Gargi's presence. Finally, with effort, she turned her face away towards the window beyond which the rain still came pouring down.

When the rain stopped, Anuradha and I stepped out. We came slowly down the stairs, trying to muffle the noise of our feet. Going past Azizun's quarters, I thought I heard the sound of *ghunghrus* and of singing. Aftab was awake and happy.

Although the street was blanketed in darkness, the sky above had turned light. It took an hour before these cliff-like houses allowed the sun to break in. In Benaras, nothing was straightforward. One was always running a hurdles race.

We passed the spot where the young man had been stabbed the other night. I told Anuradha the story and Aftab's peculiar reaction — a mixture of horror and gloating.

Anuradha maintained silence until I began to wonder if she had heard me at all.

'What do you make of Aftab?' she said all of a sudden.

'Of Aftab?' I was not ready for her question. 'I don't know,' I said at last.

'Everyone gives the same reply. "I don't know." "I don't know." I am beginning to wonder if *I* know.'

'Do you?'

'You think I don't?'

'Does he know you have been unfaithful?' I was surprised to discover that I wanted to hurt her.

'You can never tell what Aftab knows. But let me tell you one thing, Som, I have not been particularly unfaithful, not to him anyway.'

'Do you really believe that?' I asked her, astonished.

'You will not understand. I told you about my mother. My father never married her. You know that. My mother was also very religious.'

'So?'

'So? I don't know. I can only feel something inside me, like one may feel a baby, growing stronger and bigger every day. Ever since I met you I have been feeling it.'

'Feeling that you are the daughter of a religious singing woman?'

'Don't make fun of me. I have never talked like this to any one. I should not have talked to you. You are like the rest too... to...'

'Too ignorant?'

'I don't know what. And I don't want to know.'

In a burst of speechless love she clasped my hand, put it to her cheek, I kissed her hair. I was hopelessly in love with her.

A fine rain began to fall, making no effect, however, on the stream of pilgrims who filled the narrow lanes. Anuradha covered her head. With her tattooed bindi and slanting eyes she looked a bit like the women in Ajanta murals. We passed the spot where the carnival had been held the other night.

'Do you remember the juggler at the carnival?'

She did not answer but her smile left no doubt that she remembered. Again, I experienced the same sensations of frustration and jealousy that I had felt at the temple; once again I suppressed them. A little later, we reached the *ghats.* Under our feet, rain had turned the ground into slush. At every step, the slush pulled in my shoes, making a peculiar sucking sound. The slush mingled with filth, banana peels, cowdung and urine. Anuradha's chappals slipped frequently until she simply chucked them aside and stepped barefoot on to the slimy bank.

The sun, up for some time, was hidden behind the clouds. Along with the misty rain, a ghostly light fell from the sky, lighting up every stone, each decrepit shrine, the funeral pyres. The city's celebrations of the Lord's birthday were not yet ended. I could hear the sing-song of half a dozen *aaratis.* Every temple bell was being rung. Every conceivable sect was present on the mushy steps. Men and women sang, beat drums, clanged enormous cymbals, pirouetted. Hare Krishna. Hare Krishna. Hare Krishna. Hare, Hare. An American junkie, a bare skeleton, grinned: 'This is it, baby. This is it.' Indifferent to the shit under their feet, indifferent to the smell of a thousand bodies, the pilgrims jostled from step to step, ecstasy on their faces, when I would have expected disgust. Anuradha was no different. Her face suffused with a strange ecstatic glow, she muttered prayers, made offerings at every possible shrine, thought nothing if the hem of her sari got soaked in dung. The leper's guard had been doubled for the occasion. His membranes an extra red in the morning light, a tongueless boy gurgled at us from his mat of sack cloth. Anuradha bent down and put a coin on his outstretched hand, another on the stump of a noseless young woman, some more beside the knotted body of a man, his ankles flat on the ground beside his ears.

I knew, then, that I had had enough. It was this city, diseased and bankrupt, wallowing in filth and humbug, it was this city of perversions, that stood between me and Anuradha. Until I broke her from its spell, I should never succeed in completely possessing her.

We sat a few feet from an open drain our feet nearly touching the oily murky waters of the river.

'You must come and live in Bombay,' I said.

She was surprised, puzzled. 'Why do you feel that all of a sudden?'

'Some things come to you all of a sudden.'

'I can't come.'

'You don't have to worry about the expenses.'

She smiled. 'That is just like you. But I was not thinking of the expenses.'

'What else, then?'

'I can't come.'

'You mean you won't come.'

'There is Aftab.'

'You don't love Aftab. Nor does he care for you. I want you more than anything else and you can't give me a reason except to say that you can't come.'

'There are other reasons about which you do not know.'

'I don't want to know about them.'

'Don't get angry.'

She put her hand on my arm. I watched without feeling the curlicues of *mehndi.*

'Anuradha,' I said, 'I won't be coming to Benaras anymore.'

She paled as the words sank in. Tears came to her eyes.

'What have I done?'

'Nothing, darling. It is nothing you have done. I just can't stand this place.'

She clutched my arm and cried a long time wiping her tears with the end of her sari.

'I love you,' I said. 'And I don't want you to cry.'

But she cried.

~

Later that month we lay on an enormous bed in a hotel in Bombay.

'Let us run away,' I said, leaning over her.

She laughed. She had a deep, joyous laugh when she was happy. It shook her breasts and belly and I could see the fillings in her teeth.

'Men like you don't run away.'

I traced a line from her throat between her breasts, to her navel. Where other women wear marks of child-birth, she carried scars of her disease.

'What about Aftab?' I said.

She shrugged.

I looked at her. She was almost serious. My heart quickened. 'I'll come to Bombay, if you don't mind the gossip.'

'Gossip be damned.'

'Aftab has Azizun. He can always come and meet us here.'

'Are you serious?'

'Of course, I am serious. Aren't you?'

'Yes, of course.'

'You don't sound the same.'

'It always happens to me, as soon as I get something I had badly wanted. It means nothing.'

'You know what I have always felt,' she said speculatively.

'That it is not you I want and all that crap.'

She clasped me in one powerful movement and pulled me to her breast.

'I hope it is all crap, crap, crap and crap. I don't want to lose you. I would rather die.'

I fondled her hair, watching a ray of the setting sun break through the curtains. We dozed off.

When we awoke it was dark. A full moon hung just above the rim of the ocean. There were the usual neons and car lights and the blazing curve of the road. But, the moon remained undimmed. Behind me Anuradha dressed, made up her face before the mirror, gathered little odds and ends into her bag. I went up to her, put my hands on her waist, kissed the side of her throat. She watched me in the mirror. I said, 'Why do you always wear such antique clothes?'

'Maybe I am an antique person. Don't they suit me?'

'Antiqueness suits you all right.'

I turned her around. 'You are beautiful.' I said slowly, my eyes locked with hers.

'Gargi says my beauty was a screen. It is good that it was destroyed.'

'You are very beautiful,' I said.

I drove her to her aunt's home. As we passed Haji Ali she said, 'Do you think all this was bound to happen?'

'What?'

'All this that we are going through. Do you think all this was predestined?'

I was tempted to say I did not believe in the predestined business but I stuck to the truth. I said, 'I have had such a difficult time with life I don't know what to believe.'

Anuradha took my free hand, kissed the knobbly joints of my fingers.

'I had started off that evening at the Intercontinental by grabbing at Aftab's company and here we are. There must surely be some truth that connects the two.'

'I love to hear you talk like this,' she said, planting a kiss on my shoulder.

'You want me to become a second Gargi!'

'No. And Gargi does not talk!'

We drove in silence. After a while, she said, 'What are you thinking?'

'I was thinking about Lal Haveli. I had not known such places existed.'

She smiled as though to say, 'You never know that all exists in the world.'

I dropped her outside the gate of her aunt's house. She left her handkerchief in the car. I put it in my pocket. It filled the car with her strange sad perfume. I drove back leisurely, aware that my life was about to take a turn. Coming home, I sat in the silent living room, waiting for Geeta. I did not know what I was going to tell her, if anything at all. I made myself a drink and put on a record. I walked up to the large bay window. The moon shone over an empty ocean. It had grown brighter, bigger. It grew and grew, until the whole sky was in flames. Havildar, lurking in the shadows, kept an eye on me. He was the first to reach when, staggering as though at a physical blow, amidst a massive crash, I fell.

PART TWO

1

Yesterday, I went to office for the first time since I fell ill. High above the sea I sat in my room. Our offices have changed. They aren't even in the same place. My father, for twenty years, had sat in the factory. Surroundings like our present offices made him fidgety, angry. I had seen that. He had walked out of a bank because, he said, of the stench. What stench? The acrylic emulsion, the bright shiny panelling, the smell of leather? The stench of the banker's underarm? Or just the stench of money? He never answered. He was secretive about such things. But he never went to a banker again. For years we had no banker. Not until recently, when Mr. Thapar negotiated a loan for purchasing the shares of Aftab's company.

Many things have happened since that evening I collapsed on the living room floor. I was removed to intensive care. When I could be moved again I was shifted to the Maya, to this room. It at least has the second best view of the sea. The best belongs to the room where my mother spent her last days. I can't say I am dying to get into it.

The first thing K said to me after I came out of intensive care was, 'You know, Som, you ought to have died that night.'

Had I not known him better, I would have thought he wished me dead. But I agreed with him. During those last minutes of consciousness, the moon exploding behind my eyes, I had travelled terrains and registered sensations that had not belonged to any living world. I had felt then the embrace of something warm, tranquillizing, unrelenting and I had said to myself I know what this is; and I had sighed, almost in relief, until the memory of Anuradha had suddenly come back — standing before the mirror my lips against her throat — and I had fallen into a bottomless pit of despair, like a shipwrecked sailor sinking into the ocean, 'Oh shit,' I had said to myself as I drowned. 'Not now. Not now.'

'So you had given me up,' I said.

'All three of us had.'

'All three of you? Who was the third?'

'Anuradha was here.'

I stared at him, not comprehending.

'How was she here?'

'She phoned for you. Geeta told her.'

I thought for a while.

'But why hasn't she showed up since I got well?'

'I don't know.'

'Isn't it strange? Or isn't it.'

I was suddenly afraid. K leaned over and patted my shoulder. 'These drugs are depressing the heel out of you,' he said.

'There is more to this though,' I said. 'Can I go to Benaras if she doesn't come?'

'You can't do that,' K said.

'Why not?'

'You should know why not. You can phone her. I'll book a call, if you like.'

When the call came through an hour later it was Aftab who picked up the phone. He said he was sorry I had been ill. He laughed his drunken, drugged laugh and went off to get Anuradha. While I waited, I straightened up against the pillows, swallowed, put away all self-pity but when she came through and said 'Hello' in her quiet voice, all of it came rushing right back. 'Hello,' I said, unable, for the moment, to say much else.

She seemed to stop dead as though she had heard a ghost. I said, 'I have been ill. I suppose you know that.'

'Yes.'

'I thought you were to come and live in Bombay.'

'I am still in Benaras.'

'Anyway, I want to meet you. I can't come. K doesn't permit. Can you come...'

Before I had finished she broke in, 'I can't.'

I could hardly believe my ears. 'Can't what?' I said.

'Can't come to see you.'

'Why not?'

'I can't.'

'You must have a reason.'

'No particular reason.'

'Anything to do with Aftab?'

'No. No. Nothing to do with him.'

'Does he... Is he bothering you?'

'No. No.'

'Why can't you come, then, for God's sake?'

K saw my mounting anger and took the receiver from me. He listened intently. Then, he said, 'Can't you come for a day?'

I stared out at the beach in bewilderment. Surely, she would come for a day, especially if K also asked her. There was another spell of words before I heard a distinct click.

'The connection was broken,' K said, replacing the receiver.

'Why don't you say she hung up?'

'She said she is going to Europe.'

'Europe? With Aftab?'

'Yes.'

'What d'you know!' I laughed bitterly. And, here I had thought of nothing else ever since I could think again.

I had phoned her again the next morning. She had herself picked up the phone. 'Hello,' she said.

'Anuradha,' I began. There was a silence, followed by a click, as she again hung up.

Slowly, I guided the receiver back into the cradle. My hands had begun to tremble. It had happened before but nothing as bad as that. There was also a twitch at my left temple. I clasped my hands to stop them from trembling. There was nothing I could do about the twitch. If it goes on like this, I thought, I would soon be a shivering, sniffling wreck.

Her reaction had been so totally unexpected that my faculties found it impossible to grapple with it. There had to be a mix-up somewhere. But where? I could only think of Aftab. Had he discovered that we were lovers? Did he care if we were lovers? Aftab was a medieval son-of-a-bitch. You could never tell what he knew, what he cared for. A secretive devil if ever there was one. Was he threatening her? For a moment, the thought shook me up. But, then, Anuradha wasn't one to be cowed down by threats. I didn't think anyone could prevent her from doing anything that she had set her mind to. There had to be a mix up.

That afternoon, the mystery cleared up.

Geeta was putting heavy curtains in my room so I could sleep even when the sun was high. She had lost weight during the previous month.

I watched her from the depths of a terrible depression. For all my assurances to myself, the uncertainty about Anuradha was driving me insane. My chest would explode, I thought, unless I talked to someone about her. I heard myself say, 'Geeta, I have been carrying on with Anuradha.'

She continued with the curtains. For a year it had been as if she had been living away from me but she had taken over during the previous month as though nothing had happened. It was this cool strength of hers that I had always admired. She was sensible, brave, aware of certain fundamentals that lay hidden from me. There was,

I now realized, another thing. There was some subtle understanding of me, Som Bhaskar, which, too, alas, had escaped me.

She finished with the curtains, sat down next to me. 'I know,' she said, her eyes averted. I stared at her in disbelief.

'You know!'

She nodded.

I was weary of surprises. My brain could not process them. 'How do you know?'

'I guessed it when she came to see you at the hospital that night.'

'I see.'

'Some time back she wrote to me.'

'She wrote to thank you for having loaned her your husband?'

'Not that.'

After a pause, she continued, 'She wrote to say that I should forgive her and I should not mind. She said she had gone along with you because you had wanted it but it wasn't her, she said, that you really wanted.'

'Gone along with me! Gone along with me! She is talking rubbish.'

I knew my temper was getting out of hand. It had been happening frequently of late.

'You don't have to shout,' Geeta said, stiffly.

'I will shout as much as I like. What else did she write?'

'She said she will not be seeing you anymore.'

My hands started to tremble again. I grabbed them before they got out of control. The twitch had also returned. Geeta, I knew, had seen the hands as well as the twitch. My hysteria turned upon her.

'Who told you to get chummy with her, anyway?'

Annoyance flashed across Geeta's face, her mouth, her eyes, but she took hold of herself.

'Why are you upsetting yourself for nothing?' she said.

'You call this nothing.'

'I don't know what you are talking about.'

'You gang up with a loose woman. You share secrets with her. And you call it nothing.'

Geeta stared at me, horrified. 'What has gotten into you? I am going.'

And she went out.

I started to cry. Great sobs shook my body. Had I been alone in the house I would have wailed. I took a Swedish vase that stood by the bed and flung it at the wall. It fell with a terrible crash scattering flowers and broken glass. That helped. 'Screw the bitch,' I shouted at the top of my voice, reaching at the same time for a bottle of valium. Geeta came rushing in. She looked at the shattered vase, then at my tear-stained face but said nothing.

I felt better after the valium took affect. 'I can do without her,' I told myself aloud. What had pissed me off was her pretensions of unconcern, as though I were a child that she had been humouring all along. 'She had gone along with me because I had wanted it' and all that carp. And, what about our love? Her promise to come and live in Bombay? Was all that playacting? I refused to believe it, yet, there were the phone calls and there was the letter. It had either been playacting that I, in my stupidity, had taken for real. Or, she had changed her mind after this awful heart attack. Quite frankly, I told my valium-soaked nerves, quite frankly I didn't give a damn which of the two it was. For all I cared Aftab and Anuradha could go and stick it. All that concerned me was that they had made a fine fool of me, made me look like a dunce: In the eyes of Geeta, in my own eyes. They were not going to get away with it, though. Not by a long shot. I was going to settle the score sooner than they thought.

I had called Mr. Thapar that evening and told him to once again start buying the shares of Aftab's company.

The decision had not pleased Mr. Thapar. Far from it. 'Start buying them *again*,' he had said in disbelief.

'Yes.'

'What is the hurry?'

'Perhaps not for you. But I am running out of time.'

'I see.'

I could almost hear his mind hum.

'Are you serious, Som?' he said at last. His voice had acquired a new gravity.

'Absolutely.'

'You are making a mistake.'

'Mistake about what?'

'About those shares.'

'It was your idea in the first place.'

'My idea was about the shares, not about the prices. The *prices* that we first paid were high enough. Now they will be something ridiculous. They will not be worth a third of what we might end up paying for them.'

Mr. Thapar paused because he was out of breath but also to see how his advice was taken.

'I see your point,' I said cunningly.

'And what have you decided?'

'I feel we should purchase all outstanding shares — at whatever cost.'

Mr. Thapar now became very serious and stared at his nails. 'Let me inform you, then, that there is just not enough liquidity in *our* companies to do what you want me to do.'

'What do you mean?'

'There is not enough cash.'

'We can raise loans.'

'How?'

'Mortgage the lands, the plants.'

Mr. Thapar was aghast. 'But they have never been mortgaged in our entire history.'

'Well, mortgage them now.'

'I hope you know what you are doing, Som.'

'I know what I am doing.'

'Very well,' he said formally. 'If you send me the orders in writing I shall do as you say.'

That was one month ago.

~

There was a knock on the door now and Mr. Thapar walked in. He looked dapper, preoccupied.

'You need not have taken the trouble to come to the office,' he said. 'I would have come over.'

'I thought I might exercise my legs a bit.'

Mr. Thapar picked up a paper-weight in both hands and examined it for a minute.

'As you know, we have been buying shares of Aftab's company,' he began.

'Yes.'

'There is a block of shares that we can not trace.'

'Why not?'

'The block was with Aftab Rai's father. He passed them on to Mrs. Rai.'

'Anuradha?'

'Yes.'

'She is not Mrs. Rai,' I cried angrily.

Mr Thapar looked at me in bewilderment.

'Anyway, carry on.'

'The fact is that she does not have them any longer. She sold them off to someone. To whom, we do not yet know. There have been several transactions simultaneously and we have lost track of them.'

'That is very strange.'

'It happens sometimes. These shares are not on the stock exchange. It is not easy to know to whom they have been passed. I am sure we shall locate them in due course.'

'I hope the "due course" is not very long.'

'What would you like us to do. We are not detectives.'

Some part of my imagination latched on to that.

'You know, that is not a bad idea,' I said. 'Detectives are quite commonly hired these days. Even in India. Why don't we hire someone to trace those shares.'

Mr. Thapar was flabbergasted, then, quite uncharacteristically, blew up. 'I worked twenty five years with your father, you know that?'

'Of course, I do.'

'And I have worked ten years with you. It has taken thirty five years to build this business.'

He waved around the room and continued, 'If something goes wrong with this share business, we will be finished.'

'Nothing will go wrong.'

'How do you know?'

'I am sure.'

I knew I sounded like a nit-wit prince but the fact was I could not think straight. Unknown to Mr. Thapar, I was in a panic: what if this one route of settling scores with them proved a dud. I leaned forward, 'Don't you understand, Mr. Thapar. I have got to go through with this to the end.'

He stared back stubbornly.

'You are being totally unbusinesslike. I can't imagine that you are not aware of it. But I shall see what can be done.'

With that he left.

I sat back trying to control my own panic. When I could not, I stepped out.

Coming down the lift I was afraid the electricity would fail and I would be left hanging between two floors. It would not return for hours. The doors would be jammed and the air would be short of oxygen. Anything could, then, happen. The management of the building claimed they had generators hooked on, but I doubted their claim. Of late, I doubted everything and everybody.

In the foyer I approached a peon. He did not know where the generators were but his companion, the little teaboy, did. He offered to guide me. We went out through a side entrance, all the way to the back of the building. We went past the canteen, the boy announcing to his employers his business with me. Between the canteen and the building there was an opening that led to the basement. We went down a ladder. It was quite clearly not the official entrance. 'There,' said the boy triumphantly wiping his running nose on the shirt sleeve.

There it surely was. In the dusty damp cold basement it glistened with oil. I walked up to it. The engine was a six cylinder job putting out seventy horse power, may be seventy five at a crunch. And there was the alternator, a fine job in its own right. I was all admiration when I realized there were no leads, no way it could possibly be connected to the distribution system of the building. In my excitement I addressed the boy, 'The bastards have just dumped it here, just to fool us don't you see?'

The boy saw, had seen before, but did not seem worried. The problem of getting stuck in a life did not bother him.

Of late, my fears, real or imagined, had exponentially increased. I was afraid of elevators, bridges, motor cars, sea breeze, electric switches, bridges, canned food. In short, there was nothing I was not afraid of. In spite of the tranquillisers, I was always dizzy, off-balance. I took medicines for my fears but nothing happened. I knew medicines would change nothing. In my heart, I knew my fears had nothing to do with my body or with my nerves. I was afraid, I knew, because Anuradha had left me.

Coming out, I walked up the pavement towards the sea. The chauffeur watched me from the parking lot. I stepped off the kerb, pulling back the same instant, astonished by a fusillade of horns and screeching tyres. I hadn't seen the traffic light they had put up at the crossing of the main road and what used to be a lane. Someone had put up a stall for hot dogs and hamburgers. I remembered an evening when I was nine or ten. I had driven down to this point with my grandfather. He wore riding breeches, a khaki coat and a toupee. His grey moustache drooped over a full, sensual mouth. He held my hand. There was mischief in his almost blue eyes. He winked at me whenever I looked up.

The stream of cars before me was unending although I was no longer the object of their derision. The traffic lights had undergone a couple of changes without my being able to cross over. A car now braked opposite me, making me step back in a reflex. The driver and I stared at each other until I realized it was *my* car. Twisted in his seat, the chauffeur held the door open. I jumped in thinking of Tarakki and off we went through a set of amber lights.

That evening when my grandfather and I had stood at the crossing, a parade was passing down the street. My grandfather, neat, restless, mischievous, informed me it was the army that was parading. Why? I asked. They want to show off their boots and belts, that's why, he said. He patted the pocket of his breeches. I said I did not understand. Madness, he said, patting his pocket some more.

In the pocket of his breeches that evening, my grandfather carried a gun, a Colt. 38 revolver. India had been divided, rioters stalked the lanes and the alleys. My grandfather carried a gun, for protection and also out of a sense of humour.

My grandfather died a rich man. He had done his civil engineering from London, in the last year of the last century, as he put it. He gave up his job with the Public Works Department to start contracting when the city of Delhi started to get built. His idea was to cash in on the whims of the British rulers, and cash in he did.

In the fifteen minutes that I had been in the car, we hadn't moved far. There were the traffic lights of course. The offices, too were disgorging their thousands. Wind-blown men swarmed the road. A crowd of women, their sarees fluttering against the radiator pelted the bonnet of the Mercedez with groundnut shells. Everyone declared that the city was ungovernable. But the city was a monster with a life of its own. And, now, the monster had produced high-rise offices where I was certain one day to be trapped in a dead life because someone had forgotten to connect the generator.

My father avoided these high-rise offices. 'Why?' he had said when I first suggested it to him. 'Why? What have those buildings to do with us?' It wasn't rhetoric; he wanted to know. We couldn't explain to him and he continued to sit in the little room at the factory, surrounded by his journals and the fumes of chlorine.

These questions for him were elementary. He was given to bigger interrogations which he probably carried on during those nights of insomnia. Once I wandered into his room on a Sunday morning. Mother had been dead some years. He sat amidst a heap of unopened Sunday papers. I sat and smoked and read the papers. There was an item on plastics and I mentioned it to him. He did not reply. When he spoke he waved the little book at me.

'You know what it says here?'

'No,' I said.

'Just listen. "There was neither death nor immortality, then." *Then*, mind you, "nor a sign of day or night. And darkness hidden in darkness..." Have you read these... things?' I said I hadn't. He warmed up and carried on.

' "Who knows the truth? Who can tell whence and how arose the universe. The gods are later than its beginning: Who knows, therefore, whence comes this creation? Only that God who sees in highest heaven; He only knows whence came this universe. He only knows. Or, perhaps, He knows not." What do you make of this?'

'Make of what?' I said.

'Of this, for example: "Or, perhaps, He knows not." '

'I don't know what to think of it.'

'Do you think it is so: Even He does not know.'

'I don't know.'

'You had religion at Harvard, didn't you?'

'One term. They didn't explain these things.'

After a spell of silent thought my father said, 'You see, this is the problem. This is what bothers me. "Or, perhaps, He knows not." If even *He* doesn't know, then who does? Quite frankly, I don't like all this vagueness.'

He looked at me as though expecting a reply. I made none. His disappointment with the arrangement of the universe was unexpected. Perhaps it was not disappointment but creeping melancholia. Everyone has a way, a short-hand of grief.

He began again.

' "And when the sun is set, Yajnavalkya, and the moon is also set, and the fire has sunk down and voice is silent, what, then, is the light of man?" '

He did not seek my views on that. He did not even look at me. He paused, his eyes on the book and, I thought, I saw a shadow cross his face.

Nothing of all this made any sense to me, then. I was twenty two and it was not the light of Yajnavalkya that I sought. What I sought was the spotlight of the stage, red and violet and blue, hot and blinding. If, beyond their iridescence, beyond the heat and the glare, loomed the pit and the darkness of the night, it was all right by me.

It was his interrogations, I believe, that gave my father melancholia just as someone given to debauchery might contract syphilis. My grandfather, on the other hand, was a man-about-town, a gourmet, fond of women and drink. He had mistresses among the young starlets. He was a good friend but a terrible enemy, not above taking recourse to the gun. He lent and borrowed millions. Twice he lost fortunes without losing a night's sleep. Anything to do with God embarrassed him. He disappeared whenever my grandmother held *kirtans*. If he was bothered about connections he didn't go loony thinking about them. Why wasn't my father like him? Reckless, happy, unburdened by philosophical speculation. He was, of course, a scientist and had delved more deeply into truths that lie at the heart of the universe. He knew things beyond anything grandfather could imagine. Was it his knowledge, then, a knowledge of verities sparsely known among ordinary men, that had pushed him over the brink, had convinced him that there were no verities at all. And where did I fit in? I was a womanizer all right, and a boozer, but my womanizing and boozing had not settled anything. I had inherited the afflictions of both of them — for what were they if not afflictions, afflictions that had led me into unbearable entanglements. A year ago, although battered, I was getting by fairly reasonably. I had a loving wife. I worked more or less regular hours. I had ambition of sorts. And, where was I at now? I still had a loving wife. I had lost a lover whom I couldn't forget even though I was busy devising every possible stratagem that could destroy her. I was probably running down perfectly good companies. I could die any day, any moment. While I lived I made a fool of myself. For K, for Geeta, for many others I had become a pain in the ass. So where was I at? And why? Why else if not for the afflictions bestowed upon me by my genes. I was in deep trouble. And I knew it.

I reached home and went to my room. There in the rosewood cabinet I kept my grandfather's revolver which he had left me. I unlocked the cabinet and took it out of its holster. It smelled of gun oil even though it had been ages since I had oiled it. I opened the chamber. It was empty. I let out the safety catch and aiming at the windows pulled the trigger about. There was much that one could do with that gun. With a gun like that one could settle scores easily enough.

In another drawer, along with my shirts, I kept Anuradha's forgotten handkerchief. Its undying fragrance had permeated my clothing. The other night, in bed with me, her lips pressed against my shoulder, Geeta remarked at the strange perfume. It was

Anuradha's perfume, I told her, and also how it had come to be in my clothing, on my body. I had expected resentment, protest, even withdrawal. But Geeta, to my disbelief, responded with sudden powerful thrusts, as though the vision of me locked into Anuradha, was somehow more erotic to her than I by my plain self. The labyrinth, as I can see, stretches to the Maya, to Geeta, to the very edges of this beach.

Anuradha! Anuradha! My dark and terrible love.

I had thought I could do without her. The fact was I could not do without her at all. Wherever I went during the day, she stayed with me. At night I stayed up lusting after her. I tried to move my thoughts off her body, on to other things, some bit of business or my health prospects, but it was only her body that I could resurrect. I walked about the room, beyond the limits of K's permission. I tried to read. I tried listening to the radio. Strains of music would float in on the microwave. Australia, America, England, Russia. But I could not push her out of my mind. Nor could I push out that other image of hers, of her standing beside a window, tapping the panes as though she knocked at a door, staring at a purple mountain and saying, (To me? To whom?) saying in deep sorrowful tones: 'There is a god in those mountains.'

I went into the bedroom and lay down. I felt tired, high strung. Through all the humming and the arguing that went on in my head, I felt sleep coming over me.

I awoke with Geeta's car driving up the driveway, the tyres sounding off the loose manhole cover, as they always did. In her usual rapid step she came into the room. She looked grand in a light blue chiffon. She had been to the hair dresser.

K, who had been waiting for me to get up, also came in. I wondered why he had come in early today. They stood on either side of me as though unsure if I was still asleep.

'Hello,' I said wiping the perspiration off my face. K came closer. 'What is the matter?'

'I had a tiff with Mr. Thapar.'

'You shouldn't have done that,' Geeta said.

K took my pulse.

'Anything else?' he said thoughtfully, letting my arm drop.

I thought of the dream I had just had. I realized now that I had been having this dream off and on ever since I fell ill. I had had it even under the blanket of pethidine. In bits and pieces, perhaps, but pieces nonetheless of the same eerie tale. I had it the night K spoke to Anuradha on phone and she refused to come.

I sat up with effort. Why did the dream leave me so exhausted? Geeta handed me a wad of eau-de cologne.

'What is it?' K said.

'I don't know.'

A silence followed. Very far away a ship sounded its siren. I had never before heard a ship's siren this far from the harbour. I leaned out from the bed and pushed open a window. The noise of the surf immediately filled the room.

'There is a dream I keep having,' I said.

'Tell us about it,' K said.

'It is something about flying. Or, so it always seems. I am flying towards a mountain. Mountain, with a snow-covered peak. The plane is one of those yellow trainers you see at the Flying Club. I am in the front. Someone else in the back. I cannot make out who it is. The person in the back has all the gear of pilots and I cannot really see much of him. We fly through clouds and mist, we fly over hills. Endlessly. The sky above is black as pitch. As you see it in the pictures of space-flights. And all the time the mountain is there, snow-covered, towering, glowing. Even though the sky is black and there is no sun, the mountain glows. From within as it were. All of a sudden there is more mist and fog and rain. Sheets of glassy rain. I ask the man behind where the wipers are. The man laughs. ' "Planes don't have wipers," ' he says.

'Of course, they do.'

' "You are a fool," ' he says.

'But I can't see,' I tell him.

' "That's your bad luck." '

The rain beats on relentlessly.

'Where are we going ?' I ask him.

' "To the mountain, of course. Over there. Can't you see it?" '

'I can. It is very far.'

' "Not as far as it may seem," says the man.'

'Time passes. Then, I am flying again. The rain has stopped. We fly over a continuous floor of clouds. It is very cold. Cold and still. The sky is black as before.

'Where is the mountain?' I ask the man.

' "It is there," the fellow says. "Look." '

'Who are you?' I ask him.

' "Don't you recognize me?" '

'I look back and it is Aftab sitting behind me, goggles and all. He smiles in his weird way. "Look" he says again. I look at the mountain and let out a shriek. It is very close now. No farther than the sea from here. Staring me right in the face. It looks enormous. A blinding glare off its slopes. It is very close and blinding and enormous and absolutely frightening. I say to myself: it is only a dream. Presently, I'll wake up and switch on the light. But the dream carries on. I say to Aftab, 'Look, we are going to crash into the mountain'. He keeps quiet. I repeat, nearly scream into his face. And, all the time we hurtle towards that blinding peak. At a fantastic speed. Like those space crafts in the movies. I start to scream.

'Aftab still makes no reply. I turn around but the cockpit is empty. He is gone. Then I crash into it. Crash right into that blasted mountain. It was like crashing into a volcano or into the fires of the sun. I would not have thought one could dream a crash so real.'

Sitting on the bed, I shuddered involuntarily.

I stared at the dark sea and brooded. Why had it occurred so often? Was there a mystery into which everything fitted? Reality was so like an iceberg. You never saw the whole of it.

'How are you sleeping now?' K said.

'Same as before. Around two in the morning. Nothing seems to work.'

'So it seems.'

'Can't you give him something else?' Geeta said.

'We have tried everything.'

Geeta looked uncomfortable.

'Does it matter?' she said.

'I think so. I think all those hours of darkness work on his nerves. He has dreams or imagines things. Anyway, he should be out of the woods in another month.'

He discussed me as though I were not present. After a pause he addressed me: 'What is all this about detectives?' He said it gently enough but it somehow sounded harsh.

'News travels fast,' I said. 'Who told you?'

'Who would tell me?'

'Mr. Thapar must learn to hold his tongue.'

'He was only seeking my medical advice. He wanted to know if you would be terribly upset if he disobeyed your orders.'

'Disobeyed my orders?'

'Don't look surprised. You are not a pharaoh or something. Anyway, I told him not to upset you and do what you had told him to do.'

'I should think so. Anyway, I don't see how this is any of your business.'

'I am your doctor.'

'You are welcome to look after the body.'

'Those detectives are for the spirit, are they?'

He seemed worried but he smiled and I was happy to see him smile.

After K was gone Geeta and I sat in silence. She looked at me warily. It was in situations like this, when she was bothered, that she totally disarmed me. She looked so innocent and vulnerable. I wondered why she was so bothered.

'What made you hire those detectives?' she said.

'To trace those shares. Why else? Don't start worrying now.'

'I am not worrying about this thing the way you imagine.' She was annoyed. That put my back up. Havildar brought in tea for her. She took it slowly, in little sips, a frown on her pretty face. She was quite a sexy woman. She used to like sex a lot, too. Until a year ago I used to be quite jealous about her. At parties I did not mind her talking with men but I resented if she laughed too much or became too chummy. From out of this resentment I picked quarrels with her. She took such quarrels in her stride. I think she understood what was taking place. But now? Now, I thought, she too was at a loss. She didn't understand what was going on and that bothered her.

2

'Hello, Bhaskar.'

I sat drinking by the pool at the Intercontinental in Delhi. I turned to find Aftab standing behind me. I was reminded of my dream. As usual, he carried his black box. It was our first meeting since my illness, since Anuradha ditched me, which was how I usually thought of it. That morning we had had another meeting of the Plastic Manufactures' Association. I wondered if he was staying at the same hotel.

I watched him with irritation. I did not understand what it was about him that annoyed me. Or, maybe, I was only transferring to him the anger that I felt with myself. It would have been better all around if he had stayed away.

'Well,' I said. 'Sit down.'

He smiled his half-face smile.

'How was Europe?'

'Ha! You make fun of me.'

I took a large swallow from my glass. 'Not at all. It is always a pleasure to meet a true lover of Europe.'

'Between you and me, we have not been to Europe...'

'I didn't think you had,' I said contemptuously.

'We just went up to the hills and spent some time with Gargi.'

'That deaf-mute.' I was behaving like a cad but drink and despair drove me on.

'Gargi, of course, cannot speak.' He was embarrassed.

'You believe in her mumbo-jumbo, don't you?'

'I suppose it can't do you any harm.'

'Why don't you ask Gargi to help you out with your business?'

He took out a cigarette and knocked it slowly against the case.

'Why bring her into this?'

'I won't. I have had enough of her and all of you.'

Aftab kept quiet. A young English girl climbed up to the diving board. I thought of the astrologer and his prophecy. I suppose I was never going to get Anuradha. That was that. I did not want to think about her. I felt very drunk. The girl dived off the board, her legs exactly right. I drained my glass and ordered another.

'Som, you are drinking much too fast,' Aftab said.

'It's better than taking drugs.'

'If you are trying to insult me you are mistaken. I am beyond the pale. And so, in a way, are you.'

'Oh!'

'I mean it. Only a man beyond the pale can recognize another.'

'And you have recognize me?'

'Yes. I at least know what I want...'

'What's that? Drugs? Indolence?'

'A peaceful death, that is all I want. You don't even know what you want. You are being torn apart by your own doubts. Your doubts are the wolves that are going to eat you up.'

'Doubts and wolves. Fine. Very fine. You should take up poetry like your grandfather.'

He made no comment. The ice tinkling in my glass was the only sound. An age seemed to pass.

I let out a drunken chuckle. I knew I was being ridiculous. I was insulting him when, in truth, I didn't want him to leave me. He was at least someone who knew her, who saw her every day, made love to her, when he got up to go I took his hand, pushed him back into the chair.

'Don't leave me alone, for God's sake,' I cried.

Aftab sat down.

'Would you like a game of chess?' he said indicating the black box.

'I hardly know the game.'

'It will help pass the time.'

'Very well.'

It was a fine set, made of ivory, very old. I took the white pieces. My King was slightly cracked. It was obvious very soon that I was no match for him. He moved his pieces swiftly, intuitively. I was fascinated, until I remembered my loathing for Benaras, for Lal Haveli.

'You have to be more careful,' he cautioned me.

'I heard someone has taken over your company.' I had again started to bait him.

'No. Not yet.'

I castled my King.

'What if they do?'

'I can always play chess.'

'Then, there are the other distractions, of course.'

The pool was nearly deserted. It must have been getting late. Aftab spoke after a long time.

'The trouble is people like me are never taken seriously. Isn't that so, Som? Come on, admit it.'

'Perhaps.'

'We are so obviously incompetent, so... so dispensable. Who will take our confessions seriously, our pleasures, our sorrows? If we cry we are clowns. If we don't we are scoundrels. Isn't that so?'

He did not wait for my answer.

'And yet we suffer like anyone else. We dull-brained, disorganised bastards suffer the same as anyone else.'

He took my King's Bishop.

'Well, I suppose you do,' I said.

'But you don't *really* believe that. I can see it in your face.'

'I don't think you can see my face.'

'No, I cannot see your face. I have lived by other lights.'

'What lights?' I said. It was altogether a crazy, drunken exchange.

'You know the old law: God compensates you for whatever He takes away from you.'

'What have you been compensated for. Or with?'

'How caustic you are! You should have been glad to see me after such a long time. Ah, well, it does not matter. You don't mind if I smoke, do you?'

'No.'

'Now, then, what were we talking about?'

I didn't bother to remind him.

'Yes, I was telling you how God has compensated me. He has taken away everything from me. Yes, everything. Health, mind, balance. But He has given me Anuradha.'

'Anuradha!' I cried in anger. It hurt me to see him take her name. 'Anuradha! You don't much care for Anuradha as far as I can see.'

'There you are, Som. Just the thing you would say. How can one describe one's love to a man who hates so much?'

'What are you talking about?'

'Forget it. Do you believe in God, Bhaskar?'

'You know I don't.'

'In your anger you have exposed your Queen.'

I moved a piece in front of her. We went through a series of moves in silence. Instead of Begum Akhtar they were playing an old song of Sehgal: *Jangal upvan tribhuvan dhundha, par kahin na uski ter mili.*

~

Aftab spoke at last.

'Do you believe in God, Bhaskar?'

'You have already asked me that.'

'Oh yes. And you said you don't.'

'That's right.'

'God is like having a third king in a game of chess.'

'Oh!'

'Do you believe in the tantras?'

'What tantras?'

'You have to sacrifice before you are given. You can't have your cake and eat it, too.'

'Oh!'

'That is what you insist on doing. I know you want to believe.'

'Believe?'

'You want to have faith. But you also want to reserve the right to challenge your own faith when it suits you.'

I was suddenly interested. Not as much because of what Aftab was saying as by his manner. His whole bearing had undergone a change. He was neither laconic nor self-conscious. I had never seen him like that.

'Am I not right? Don't you want to have your cake and eat it, too?'

'What is wrong with that?'

'It destroys you.'

'I don't see how.'

'Ah, time will tell. Time will tell. I am afraid you are going to lose your Queen, after all.'

'I am in love with your wife, you know,' I said, making the next move. I clowned even though my heart was bursting.

'Yes, yes. Check.'

His Queen was attacking my King.

'I am serious, Aftab.' Why was I so insistent? Did I expect him to become a go-between and bring her back to me? 'Everyone loves her,' said Aftab. If I was being ridiculous he was exasperating. 'I don't love her like that,' I nearly shouted but thought better of it.

'Tell me: Why can't you run your company?'

I wanted to humiliate him, to make him whine. I was ashamed of what I was doing and yet I could not stop.

'I don't know,' was all that he said.

'Anuradha is no doubt cleverer than you.'

'No doubt,' he said, readily agreeing. 'The Queen always is. Check.'

I studied the board. There was no way I could save my King. I surrendered.

We sat back in silence. The swimming pool was deserted. A lone African, in full regalia, sat at the bar.

'If only I were not so tired,' cried Aftab, pathetically, his mood suddenly shifting.

'Tired?'

'If only I could start life again.'

I understand what you mean, I wanted to say, but I was too bent upon insulting him. I said, 'I don't think you will do any better even if you started again.'

'Better? I was not thinking of that. What is the time?'

'Almost midnight.'

'I must go,' he said starting to pack in the pieces.

On the spur of the moment I wanted to say to him, 'Please take me with you,' but my pride prevented me. I said 'Give me a fag, will you. One of your hand-rolled jobs.'

He carried them in a slim gold-plated case. He was a dandy where such things were concerned.

Smoke soothed my nerves but a moment later opened up all the wounds. I could see the room, the coloured ventilators, and Anuradha lying naked on the peacock-carpet, her make-up smudged with perspiration, her mouth open, dry and hot, uttering such deep-throated cries that I had to cover it with my hand lest she might be heard.

'Anuradha asked me to give this to you,' Aftab said.

'Thanks,' I said.

I stretched out my hand mechanically. Aftab stood up.

'When do you leave?'

'Tomorrow morning,' Aftab said.

I took a moment to rev up my courage, swallow my pride. 'Can I come with you?' I managed to say.

For a moment, he was too surprised to speak. Then he shouted. 'No. No. Never.'

He stalked off towards the lobby.'

'Damm you,' I cried to his disappearing back.

I sat back, turning Anuradha's package in my hand. It was curiously heavy for its size. I tore it open. A shining object fell to the floor. I picked it up with unsteady hands. It turned out to be a little silver Krishna, flute and all. A brief note in her hand said, 'I got this from Gargi. You must always keep it with you.'

I sat by the pool, drunk, sleepless. The bar had closed or I would have got another drink. I had whisky in my room but did not have the energy to move. I poured the silver Krishna from one hand to the other. He carried her perfume. That was the only gift that Anuradha had ever given me. I couldn't possibly throw it away. Like Aftab I, too, had wanted to start life all over again. What would have I done with it, though? What indeed?

3

Today, Mr. Thapar came to see me. After he was gone I wandered back to my room, mesmerized, staring in disbelief at the detectives' report that he had left with me. Geeta passed by on her way to the bath. She came to me noticing, perhaps, the look on my face. I handed the report to her. It was a mistake but I had been too off-balance to guard against it. The fact was that I had been caught totally by surprise.

I watched Geeta's face. She paled but said nothing.

'Isn't it funny?' I said.

'I don't see what is funny.'

I laughed.

'You have got to have a sense of humour, Geeta.'

'I don't see what humour has to do with this. Anyway, what do you plan to do?'

'I will have to go to the mountains.'

'Yourself?'

'I think so. It could get complicated.'

'Everything is so complicated as it is,' she said at last and went on to the bath.

At lunch, unexpectedly, K dropped in. I sat in a cane chair on the verandah overlooking the beach. Geeta sat beside me. The beach was empty except for two men and their wives trying to set afloat a small sail boat. The boat was painted a bright post-office red with a white band running along the rim. I had a headache. Geeta went up to meet K. He waved to me as he came up. I realized Geeta must have asked him to drop in.

'So you are at last laughing again,' he said.

I grinned.

'I want to give you the good news,' I said. 'Maybe Geeta already has.'

'She hasn't. What is it?'

'They have located those missing shares.'

'Who have?'

'The detectives.'

'Oh!'

'They are lying with Krishna.'

'What Krishna?'

'The god, man, the god, who else!'

K was dumbfounded.

'No less a man than Krishna is holding the shares of Aftab's company.'

'It is ridiculous. Where are they?'

I gave him the report.

After he had glanced through it, K looked at me and at Geeta and then back at me. He said, 'What is next?'

'Next we get hold of them, what else?'

'Can't you do without them?' Geeta said, her voice barely audible.

I made no reply.

'Have you bought them? Actually bought them? Have you?' said K.

'Mr. Thapar is negotiating with the secretary of the temple.'

'What do you think of all this?' Geeta asked K.

'I have no head for such things.'

'I did not mean the business angle.'

'I don't think I am interested in any angle.'

There was a new distaste in his voice.

'You can't take this attitude when Som is ill, K.'

'Oh, can't I?' K said with unexpected vehemence. 'Som doesn't think he is ill at all. Just look at him. Smiling away like a king. Just hear him laugh. He can't sit still, he is laughing so much.'

I had been watching the couples trying to put the boat out to sea. Every time they did it the boat came back after a few flutters. In fact, they were doing it all wrong. The sails were wrong. The ropes were wrong. I did not think they were ever going to put the boat out. But, then, they did not know it.

As I watched them quite an unconnected thought entered my head. I thought of how people's lives run smoothly, successfully for years and then they do something unusual, take a wrong turn, make a stupid decision, and everything goes to pieces.

K sipped the coffee which Havildar had brought. Geeta looked at him, trying to figure him out. I was myself astonished at his bitterness. I hadn't slept well and I hated being dragged into arguments as Geeta, I felt, wanted to do. For the moment I had developed an allergy to arguments. All I wanted was silence.

'But why?' K burst out suddenly, incoherently.

Geeta started.

'Why? Why?' K repeated.

I could hear Havildar talking to the gardener in a shrill voice.

'Why what?' Geeta said at last, more nervous than ever.

'Why these riddles?'

'Riddles?'

'There is something going on here. Something more than the buying and selling of shares. I think you know what is going on. So does Som. So do Aftab and Anuradha. Poor Thapar probably is the only one who does not know. And I am another.'

'I certainly do not know what is going on,' I put in.

'Anyway, I want you to leave Anuradha alone,' K said.

'Leave Anuradha alone? I wish she had left me alone.' I burst out, trying to control my temper. 'In any case,' I continued, 'this has nothing to do with her. We have bought all the other shares and we are going to buy these. There aren't two ways about it.'

After a long silence during which all of us seemed to watch the couples with the sailboat, Geeta said, 'K Som wants to go to the mountains.'

'He must be out of his mind,' K said. 'And why does he want to go to the mountains?'

'To get those shares.'

K turned to me.

'Why can't Thapar go?'

'I want to meet Krishna personally,' I laughed. 'That's why.'

K addressed Geeta. 'Do you realise what his going to the mountains means?'

She nodded. K flared up again.

'No, you don't. He is going to die climbing those mountains looking for those shares. He is going to die, that's what it means.'

'That is why I thought you should go with him,' said Geeta. She had become very tense.

'I am afraid I cannot be a party to this hounding of Aftab and Anuradha,' K said.

'You mean you won't go with him.'

'I mean exactly that.'

Geeta started to cry.

'This is a cheerful group,' I said, trying to laugh it off.

'We are all very pleased at your having acquired Aftab's company,' said K.

I bowed in mock acknowledgement.

'It is all very simple,' I said.

'Good luck,' and K got up to leave.

~

Of course, it was not simple. I knew that the moment I had set eyes on the detectives' report.

After everyone was gone — Geeta to her room, K back to the town — I took out an old pipe and a tin of smoking tobacco. The tobacco had dried a bit — I had bought it at Hong Kong a year earlier — and kept spilling out of the bowl of the pipe. When it was finally packed I went out and sat on the mound on the beach. I blew out several great puffs of blue smoke. Then the pipe went out and I put it down.

No, there was nothing simple about this thing. There was nothing simple about Krishna. Had it been so, He would not have survived ten thousand years. He would have died along with the gods of the Pharaohs, the Sumerians, the Incas. Krishna was about as simple as the labyrinths of Aftab's Haveli.

PART THREE

1

I am back from a bizarre mission in the mountains. Back to the surf, the insomnia. To this minute-book to which I am as badly addicted as Aftab is to his cigarettes. The high-rise offices are back, too. Mr. Thapar has troubles and he wants me daily at the office.

One misty morning, a month ago to the day, K and I sat beside a whirling stream that ran at the foot of the Guest House where we waited for the mountain-road to open. (K had come with me, after all, although I could not say what exactly had persuaded him at the last minute?) On the other side of the stream lay a vast boulder strewn expanse. Mist hung over the stream and the boulders. Beyond them, across a cold mountain, in an adjacent valley, lay our destination.

Like a vaporous halo, the mist hovered around K who sat on a boulder ahead of me. I knew he was worried about my health. He expected me to drop dead any minute. So, at times, did I. That is the trouble with heart problems. You lived from millisecond to millisecond. You never know what is coming next.

We had been waiting at the Guest House for two days. The road ahead was blocked with landslides. It was anyone's guess when it might be opened to the traffic. The wait had been working on our nerves until we were barely on speaking terms.

Through the swirling mist, K strolled back towards me. I said, 'On a sunny day, when the mist clears, you can see the mountains.'

'I can't say I am dying to see them,' he replied as he sat down next to me. 'Look, Bhaskar,' he said. 'Are you sure you want to go through with this?'

'Why not... when we have come thus far.'

'The toughest bit lies ahead.'

'Don't worry. If I survived the heart attack, I shall survive this.'

'You haven't a clue how you survived the heart attack.'

'What do you mean?'

'Never mind. Let us fish while we are here,' he said suddenly.

'We haven't got the equipment.'

'They rent them out in a shop in the market.'

As we walked towards the market, K asked, 'What is on that mountain, anyway?'

'I don't know.'

'A temple?'

'Maybe. Maybe a cave. Maybe just a stone. God knows what.'

The little man at the shop was all flurry and obsequiousness. Tackles? Yes, he had the best tackles in the world. K picked one and moved out into the sunlight. He stood trying it out thinking of something else.

'I hope the damn thing works,' he said.

He was irritated. Little, unexpected obstacles had been irritating him during the trip.

We went back to the stream with the fishing tackles. The mist had begun to lift although it was not quite clear yet. Somewhere in the sky, invisible to us, the sun battled his way. The light varies intermittently. We lowered the lines. We sat far apart, in tacit agreement to avoid conversation. I had seen a couple of trouts, although I doubted if we could catch anything in that swift current.

Sitting there, I thought of good old Leela and her friend Descartes. 'I think, therefore, I exist.' Every thing could be reasoned out, she said. And I was on my way to reason out Krishna Himself. Descartes should have approved. Of course, Descartes was no agnostic. He granted the existence of God. Since the idea of God existed in men's minds, he reasoned, it must have been God himself who had put it there in the first place. But the times had changed. Things were not so simple anymore. Children were brought up to believe they were born with blank minds. They were brought up to challenge everything. Whatever, ultimately, filled their minds first to be proven *de nova*, personally reasoned out. People had put their faith in too many things — monarchies, nation-states, decency of man, God — only to discover that they had been led up the garden path. They were not willing to take anything for granted. So the children of the West grew up doubting everything. And, now, it had come to the East, along with Coca Cola, IBM and the English language. I could see it all too clearly in my own case, even in my father's case. Except that his faith in reason seemed to totter towards the end. Faith in reason was, after all, also a faith. Why not faith in a god? Was that what this ass-breaking trip was really about? To know if God existed? Surely, if He could hold shares, He could give other evidence of His existence.

Another thought crossed my head. I toyed with it, wondering whether to tell K. Why was I being secretive about it? Could it be that I saw in what I had discovered at the Guest House a day earlier, a clue to the bigger puzzle of the trip itself and I did not want to share it with anyone lest the mystery be destroyed. I decided, finally, not to tell K. Anyway, he would probably put it aside as just one more dream.

After a long interval, K said, 'I don't suppose we shall catch anything.'

'We can go back whenever you like,' I said.

'Let us go back *now*,' he said impulsively, pulling in the line.

We went back. K looked discouraged. I did not know what discouraged him. He wanted to sleep. I sat in an easy chair on the verandah, watching the dark lowering sky. There was thunder across the valley. It started to rain. The wind whipped the rain into a frenzy until I could see neither the boulders nor the stream. The rain beat on the tin roof of the Guest House. Lulled by its drumming, I dozed off.

It was late afternoon when I awoke. The roar of the stream filled the air. I walked down to it. It had swollen magically during the rain. The boulders we had sat on, were now islands several feet inside the stream. The sky was lighter, brighter, more hopeful. I decided to walk over to the tourist office and find out about the road.

At the Tourist Office, a bespectacled woman sat at the counter, knitting socks. On the wall behind her, on a large poster, rose a mountain range, the snow of its peaks shining in the sun. The woman refused to lift her eyes from the socks. 'Are you in charge here?' I asked.

For some reason this seemed to offend her. 'What do you want?'

'I want to speak to the Manager.'

'I am the Manager,' she said, although she obviously was not.

'I want to know about the road.'

'What about it?'

'When is it being opened?'

'How are we to know?'

'Who is supposed to know?'

The girl who sat at the typewriter looked up. 'If it clears up, the road will be opened,' she informed.

'It may not clear up for six months,' said the woman who thought herself the manger.

'You don't say!'

'In that case you will have to come next year.'

She grinned as though that was the happiest information she could give us. I turned to the typist.

'Do you know anything about this shrine?' I gave her the name.

'It is a well-known place,' said the typist.

'Do you know who lives there?'

It was a silly question. I drew a blank. 'You must have some leaflets about it, some photographs.'

'I'll see,' said the typist. She went to the back of the room, opened a rickety old cupboard and started to rummage through a dusty heap of papers. I sat down in a chair with a broken arm. Clickety-clack of the needles filled the room. The 'manager' scowled at me and her assistant by turns. An anaemic shaft of sunlight came in through the door and lit her heavy throat and jaw. Was the sky clearing up? My eyes wandered away from her and came to settle on the poster. I had a feeling I had seen it before. There was no caption to it. I must have stared at the poster a long time. The light had now shifted from the woman's throat to her face. It was glinting off her spectacles. At the back of the room the typist quietly rummaged through the files. My gaze went back to the poster.

Finally, the typist gave up.

'I am afraid we have nothing on it.' She seemed genuinely sorry.

'I told you so,' said the sock-knitter.

'Maybe, you will have some next year,' I said.

'You came here last year,' said the typist suddenly.

She took me by surprise. I did not know whether it was a question or a statement. I kept quiet. 'Did you know the woman who was staying at the Guest House?'

'What woman?'

'She came here once to ask about the road. She said she wanted to take you there. How is she?'

'Good bye,' I said. 'And thanks for the information.'

I started for the Guest House; then, on the spur of the moment, turned towards the mule-post. The proprietor was all salaams and smiles.

'Mules, sir?'

'Yes.'

'When do we start, sir? Tomorrow?'

'As soon as the road opens.'

'It will open tomorrow,' he declared confidently.

I started to move away, then turned back.

'Listen,' I said, 'What do you know about this temple?'

'Everything, sir.'

'Who lives there?' I mean who is in charge?'

'It is a big temple, sir. Many people are in-charge.'

I gave up.

'Anyway, we leave tomorrow if it clears up.'

Coming back, I walked beside the stream. I thought of the several summers that as a boy I had spent in similar mountains. My mother was alive then, young and beautiful. It had been a charmed world. After her death, I had passed another vacation in the hills, but the charm was gone, leaving in its place an unbearable loneliness. Until that summer with Anuradha, I had avoided the hills. That summer had left scars of its own.

A passing peasant, a bundle of faggots on his back stopped me for a light. Backing up against a rock he lowered his burden, eyeing me all the while. I lit his cheroot for him. He took a couple of puffs, 'You were here earlier,' he said.

'Three days ago.'

'No. A year ago.'

Once again, I was surprised. I looked at him closely. I could not place him. I did not know what to say.

'You stayed at the Guest House.'

I felt the stirrings of alarm as though a secret was about to be ripped off.

'How do you know?'

'I saw you with your wife.'

I kept quiet.

'People said she was not your wife. But she was beautiful.'

I turned and left. The sun disappeared behind some clouds. I came to a wooden bridge but walked on. There was another bridge further up. I knew. As the peasant said, I had been here before. This was the place where Anuradha and I had come the year before. We had stayed in the same Guest House, in the same room. During the afternoons, I had walked along the same stream, my arm around her shoulders. Above me, to the left, there was the copse of pines where, under a bright blue sky, I had made love to her. Later, blushing, filled with wonder, she had said, 'I had never imagined it like this.'

Nor had I.

Those were six unbelievable days snatched somehow from the hands of eternity. Or, was it from the hands of Krishna?

I did not understand why I had not told K about my visit here. I had come close to telling him that morning. Perhaps, it was the desire to cover up my trail. But why? And trail to where? Had I superstitions? Was I afraid a spell would be broken?

It was getting late. A continuous stream of peasants, wood and children on their backs, met me coming from the other direction. I wondered how many of them recognized me. I came to the last bridge. It was deserted, dark brown, a little creaky. As I started to cross, I noticed the boy. He had walked down to the edge of the stream. He wore a yellow high-neck pullover and a red corduroy cap. I had seen him at the Guest House earlier. They had probably arrived that morning. He knelt beside the stream, one knee higher than the other. He had pebbles in one hand that he held, by turn, against the sky. He was thirteen or fourteen. Fair, very good looking.

'Hello,' I shouted above the din of the stream.

He waved to me.

'What are you doing?'

He could not hear me. I walked on.

I looked at the sky. A yellow light suffused it. It grew in intensity. In the west, the overcast had dissolved. The light of the setting sun came in sharp and clear. The clouds were swiftly moving away, exposing an orange-green sky. The light could not last long but the sun, the next day, I knew, would come out bright and strong and the road would be opened.

2

It was cold the next morning but the sky had cleared. There was a hint of mist but it did not last. K wore a heavy cricketing sweater with the colours of the Bombay University. I, too, had dug out a wind-cheater. The road before us was treeless and empty. I wondered what could have made it so totally without vegetation because the altitude was not such where nothing would grow. There was the mountain to the left of us and boulders to the right. If we stood between two boulders we could look down a steep drop of hundreds of feet, at the bottom of which lay a valley. The green of the valley was overlaid with a blue haze. In the centre of it meandered a stream. From this distance it was no more than a shining thread of silver. We were followed at a distance by the mule driver and his mules.

We walked in silence. K looked preoccupied. I knew what he thought of the journey and did not want to revive a new debate. It did not occur to me that he might have problems of his own. Anyway, I too needed the silence. What with the medicines and the waiting, my nerves were on edge and needed to settle down.

A couple of hours later the valley had disappeared, its place taken by a narrow gorge. The stream was still there but the green terraced fields were gone. The gorge was not as deep as the valley. At times, I could hear the whirl of the stream. It was swifter here. As it rushed by, it made little waterfalls. We were probably approaching its source.

And now we noticed a cluster of men on the road ahead. They were dressed in bright ochre robes and walked with a curious lopsided gait as though running a three-legged race. Slowly, we gained upon them. The narrow path had begun to twist and turn. The ochre men were visible one minute, gone the next. Then, suddenly, we ran into them, nearly crashed into the litter that they were carrying. The object that had jogged so awkwardly ahead of us was not, after all, men but a *palki* with ochre flaps. It was small and narrow and was meant for such mountainous journeys. It was carried by two men who were relieved by another pair every other mile.

Women still observed purdah in these parts! Two silent men — one of them a priest — followed at a distance. Next to the litter itself I recognised the young boy whom I had seen on the river bank. He, too, walked in silence, hands locked behind his back. He wore the same yellow pullover and corduroy cap.

'Hello,' I said as I came level.

He looked up, broke into a grin. The smile brought out the child that he was.

'Are you going to the shrine?' I said.

'We are going to the lake?'

I wondered where that was.

'Is that your mother in the *palki?*'

'Oh no! It is my grandfather. We are taking him to the lake. We shall reach there this evening.'

The boy and I walked on ahead. K fell in with the *palki.* We walked some distance in silence. The boy hummed a song. I said, 'What were you doing at the stream yesterday?'

'I was looking for pebbles.'

'Pebbles?'

'A special kind of a pebble.'

'Did you find it?'

'I did not. But I want to look again on our way back.'

'It is not easy to find the kind of pebble I want,' he added with some pride.

'What kind of pebble is that?'

He stared at me as though appraising me. 'I have not told anyone but I will tell you.'

'Thanks.'

He nodded. 'I am looking for pebbles that you can see right through, you understand? You can see right through them even if they are stones. You can see through them as you can see through glass. And in the centre of the stone,' here he squinted through an imaginary stone, 'in the centre of the stone is a star.'

I looked at him in wonder.

'Who told you all this?'

'My grandmother.'

'And what if you don't find the pebble?'

'Even then it is all right.'

My God, I thought, here was another Pascal. The thought depressed me. What depressed me was that a child so young should have been contaminated in such a manner. This, too, was corruption, although of a different sort. For all one knew, he would spend the rest of the days searching for a crystal pebble with a star. And become a nut in the process.

We talked of other things. They were from Jaipur, a family of jewellers. His grandfather was not well. The man walking beside the litter was his uncle. The other was the family priest. His father had stayed behind to mind the shop. He studied in the seventh class.

'What do you want to become when you grow up?'

'I'll sit in the shop,' he replied without hesitation.

So, that was that. I introduced myself. 'I am from Bombay,' I said. 'I make plastic buckets. I have two very young daughters. Have you been to Bombay?'

'No.'

'Have you ever seen the ocean?'

'No.'

'Don't you want to?'

'Yes. But I don't mind if I don't.'

Suddenly, the boy asked me, 'Where are you going?' His large brown eyes were clear and shiny.

'To the shrine, I hope.'

'You want to take a vow?'

'Oh, no.'

'Then?'

I hesitated.

'I have to pick up something.'

'*Prasad?*'

'No. No. I have to gather some shares. You understand shares?'

He did not and I did not care to elaborate.

We had been climbing steadily. In spite of the cool breeze the sun was sharp. Little bits of snow stuck to the boulders on either side of the road. There were no tress or bushes or birds or flowers. It was a barren moonscape, a volcanic eruption that had swallowed all except the rocks. The gorge to the right of us was as deep as before.

We paused by a little stream. I wanted to wash my face but the water was icy. The stream fell a few feet, disappeared under the road, then emerged on the other side to make a sharp waterfall. We climbed a boulder and waiter for the others. It was nearly noon. I was hungry. The boy put on a pair of dark glasses. I thought of Aftab.

In the distance I could hear the song of the *palki* bearers. It was an odd sound in the stillness. K and the *palki* arrived a little later. The *palki* went by without stopping. The boy's uncle paused briefly to take him along. The two of them hurried after the disappearing litter.

'Very strange,' said K after they were gone and the sing song of the porters had died out.

I said, 'There is his sick grandfather in that litter, the boy told me.'

'I know.'

K sat beside me where the boy had been. He did not look any the worse for the journey, just thoughtful. The mule arrived with the food.

We ate with relish. There was beer that the mule driver had picked up in the town.

'If we don't consider your share-nonsense it is not a bad trek,' K said.

'But you shouldn't consider my share-nonsense.'

'I wouldn't if it were not so badly entangled with so much else.'

After a pause he continued, 'There are so many things that I can't figure out. Here are these shares, for example, quite worthless according to Thapar but you are bent upon acquiring them. I can't imagine you are not aware of what Thapar thinks of them. Then, there is the strange manner in which these shares have travelled. There is Aftab. I can't understand his silence,' I thought of my meeting with him in Delhi. 'Above all, there is Anuradha,' K said.

'Yes, what about her?' I said, my heart picking up a bit.

K looked up sharply. 'That name does work on you, doesn't it? Are you still in love with her?'

I kept quiet.

'I suppose you don't know.'

'That's right. I don't.'

I watched the silent barren hills around us. Had the time come to share other things with K?

'You know,' I said, 'for many years now, I have had this awful feeling that I wanted something. But the sad thing was it didn't make the slightest difference when I managed to get what I had wanted. My hunger was just as bad as ever. A year ago, I couldn't imagine, a wish, which if fulfilled, would have made the least difference to my life. You know all this. Then came Anuradha. It could be that she made an impression on me because she was so different from the women I had known. So, at least, I thought in the beginning. Later, it became more confused. There was more to her than met the eye. A world spinning all by itself. I was infatuated with this mysterious world. Here was a woman, I thought, who could make a difference to me, to my life. The more I took of her, the more I wanted. Until, of course, she ditched me in this awful manner and I felt like a dunce.'

K shrugged. 'You could be romanticizing, you know. Blowing things larger than life.'

'Possibly.'

'But there is something about Anuradha... Pass me another beer, will you?'

I opened it for him the wrong way. We watched the foam bubble down the sides. After a couple of swallows K said. 'You know, Som, my life had been spent amidst misery and suffering but I know of no other human being who suffered as much as Anuradha.'

I looked at him in surprise. That was oddly sentimental stuff to come from K.

'You know much about her?' I said.

'I know enough. Illegitimate child, insane mother, no home. Molested as a child. Witness to murders, suicides, every conceivable evil of the world. Can you imagine what a childhood she must have had?'

'I don't know everything about her.'

'You don't think she is an industrialist's daughter, do you?' K snapped.

'Not that but...'

'Anyway, from all that, she is suddenly plucked out and put in a convent. Even the gutter is denied to her. Such desperate loneliness amidst all those priggish daughters of the well-to-do. All those years she does not make a single friend. She thinks only of her dead, insane mother. She comes out. Her aunt manages to put her on the screen, probably makes a neat packet for herself in the bargain. A couple of producer types paw her now and then but there is a year or two of success. Then Aftab comes along.'

'What she saw or sees in him is a mystery to me.'

'What she saw in him was Gargi. It was to Gargi that she was drawn.'

'To Gargi?'

'Yes. Not that Aftab was not an attraction in himself. None of this goggles stuff at the time. An impressive horseman. A polo player of sorts. They had a stud farm. Then there was his father, an imposing figure, a true gentleman. Anuradha was happy for a couple of years. Then Aftab's father died and Aftab went to pieces right before her eyes. She lost her looks and tried to kill herself. There was endless humiliation. Misfortunes piled, one upon another. You see?'

He did not look at me.

'Do you consider me one of the misfortunes?'

'I am afraid I do,' he said with a sigh. He got up, dusted his trousers as though getting rid of me. A little later, we were on our way.

~

We arrived that evening on a narrow ridge, high in the mountains, and the first thing I saw through the settling dusk was the bright ochre of the litter. It sat in the yard of a ramshackle hut. There was no sign of the boy or his uncle although I could see two of the porters squatting a little distance away. We camped in a similar tumble down room. I sat on the steps, smoking, while K washed up. From now on, the journey would be downhill. A space had been cleared in front of the huts. A little shrine, waist high, faced the huts, housing a vermillion daubed statuette. Someone had lit an oil lamp at its feet. Beyond the shrine, as far as I could see, stood enormous boulders, as though piled in a hurry by a giant hand. Beyond the boulders, I supposed, were more mountains, endless valleys. Even as I looked, night fell. It came down with the abruptness of a faulty stage curtain. It was dark before I had finished my cigarette.

After dinner, K and I sat sipping brandy, exchanging an occasional word. Had K told me all he knew about Anuradha? I could ask but I knew I would get nowhere. K talked in his own good time.

I do not know what awoke me that night. A drop in the temperature? The scampering of a rat? There was a high wind. I lay in my sleeping bag listening to its howl. Above the rush of the wind, I thought I heard a muffled chant. It came as though carried down from a great distance, like the imaginary chant among the voids that I had heard all my life. But there was nothing imaginary about this one. I sat up and listened more carefully. From his side of the dark room K said, 'It is the old man.' He was already out of his bed, pulling on his boots. I followed suit. As we stepped out of the room the chaste Sanskrit hit us in the face. The other hut had come alive. A knot of men stood near the litter holding lanterns. Their shadows, long and tremulous, did an eerie dance against the crumbling walls of the hut. I looked at K.

'I think the old man will die now,' K said.

'The boy's grandfather?'

'Yes.'

'What do you mean he will die now?'

'There is a lake somewhere here. He has come to die near it.'

'He has travelled nine hundred miles to die near a lake!' I said in a amazement.

'So it seems.'

We now moved towards the lights. They had transferred the old man to a cot. He lay with his hands crossed over his chest. His face, gaunt and austere, was nothing but bones. There was life yet in the eyes, though. Slowly, they travelled in an arc over the faces that surrounded him. As his gaze passed over me I had the unreasonable impression that he recognized me. He lingered a little longer over his son and his grandson, then his eyes closed. The porters picked up the cot. The priest led the way. At the tail end, K and I joined the little procession. The impenetrable looking wall of boulders now opened to reveal a path that snaked gently down. At the head, the priest resumed the recitation. The immaculate Sanskrit echoed against the cold rocks. The crowd of porters at the back muttered their own prayers. And then, quite suddenly, K stumbled to a halt.

'My God, Som, look at that!'

We had cleared the boulders and stood on a narrow ledge. A nearly full moon hung above. Directly below us, at the bottom of a precipice, lay the dark surface of a lake. Its waters had the smoothness of black glass. Steep cliffs, bronze in the moonlight, arose all around its circumference, as if guarding it from an evil eye. Beyond the cliffs, towering above them, rose a snow covered peak. This was the mountain that I had seen on the poster in the tourist office. I froze as I realized why it had appeared familiar. This was also the mountain of my nightmare. There was a movement in the lake, and now I became aware of a break in its glass surface. It seemed as though there was an island floating in the dark waters. It seemed to heave, move slowly towards us and, then, as it came nearer, K, his voice wonderstruck, whispered, 'It's a glacier, Som.'

The party had passed on, their chant trailing behind them. I stood petrified staring at what lay before me. I had seen lakes and glaciers before but such was the total effect of the scene that I felt shaken to the core. I felt I had been here before. The sense of *deja vu* left me numb.

We could no more hear the priest. We waited and watched the glacier approach. Directly below us it seemed to pause, and through blind glazed eyes look up at us, two strangers from another world. I stared, fascinated.

The glacier floated away. We hurried on. The path, chalk white in the moonlight, dipped sharply. The same moonscape prevailed here. No vegetation, or animals or reptiles or birds. Only the vagrant wind, black waters, bronze cliffs in the shadow of the mountain, a blind glacier gliding from one end to the other, keeping guard on the gates of whatever it was that lay beyond.

We caught up with them at last, just as they were putting the old man down next to the waters. A hush fell. The priest whispered something in the old man's ear and turned his face towards the mountain and those unbelievable cliffs. I wondered what his dying eye saw. Did he see the vision of the other world that, like a cosmic magnet, had drawn him over a thousand miles? We settled down now for the vigil. K stood with the uncle. The boy and I sat on a rock as we had done during the afternoon. The porters sat huddled a little distance away. The priest sat by the cot performing the rituals, whispering to the old man.

I wondered what we were doing there, what I was doing there, I who had always avoided funerals. I marvelled at the boy's wondrous equanimity. He watched the proceedings through large alert eyes, as if it was a play and not a real funeral. Did he realize that this was Death? For that matter, did I? Maybe that was where the trick lay. Along with the old man we had all travelled to the other world, chanting, free from fear. You might as well be afraid of a train travelling from one station to another. That black lake, those bronze cliffs, were certainly another station.

One after another, as if by agreement, each one of us fell silent. I looked around and somehow I knew that the old man's hour had come. Everyone else knew that, too. Once again the priest's chant rose on the still air, each syllable carved out of stone like the notes of Azizun's songs. And if her songs had delineated all of life's possibilities, these hymns outlined those of death. The porters moved a little distance away and started to build a pyre. K and I carried a log or two just as we had done for my father. When all was ready, the dead man, cot and all, was carried to the pyre which was lit by the son. The wood, crackled and burned filling the air with incense. The flames leapt against the rock and also in the mirror of the lake and in the tearful eyes of my young friend. He had been especially close to his grandfather I learnt later.

3

We arrived the next evening in a town on the curve of a hill. The descent had been steady, in a series of spirals. The surroundings had gradually turned green. Trees, flowers and birds had reappeared. We had entered the valley that Anuradha had spoken of.

We sat at a tea shop in the bazaar. It was a narrow street. One could conceivably have nailed two planks and walked from one wooden balcony to another. There were people on the road and in the balconies, good-looking but dirty, in *churidars* and peculiar caps. They looked us over briefly. They were quite used to tourists in this town. It was, after all, at the junction of several sacred routes. There was dust everywhere, and flies. There was no sign of snow. 'Have you been here, as well?' K said. I had told him the previous night, after the old man's cremation, how Anuradha and I had spent a week in the Guest House.

'No,' I laughed. 'I was urged to, though.'

'Urged to? By whom?'

'By Anuradha. I refused.'

K looked tired.

'Where is this place where your shares are?'

'I don't know. We shall ask.'

But we were too tired to make a move. We waited for the mule driver who had disappeared, waited for something to happen. The street rose steeply away from us. Half an hour later the mule driver appeared at the top of the street. Accompanied by an old *panda*, he threaded his way through the crowd. The *panda* was handsome and tall but nonetheless, a *panda*. The mule driver said the Forest Guest House was full. There were, however, little private lodging houses. While we debated the matter the handsome old *panda* introduced himself. What he said was unexpected.

'Shrimanji,' he said, 'your father came here twenty years ago and he had the same problem. The Forest Guest House was full. So was

the P.W.D. Guest House. I went with him everywhere. I said to him: Bhaskarji, I am your servant. My forefathers have looked after your ancestors for two hundred years. I am poor but can my humble hut not hope to house you for two nights.'

I was speechless with surprise. The *panda* had to be bluffing as, I was told, they always did. I turned to K. The expression on his face was not of surprise but of a sudden alert. A mule train passed, jingling bells, spreading an extensive stink. When the bells had died I said, 'This is very strange. Do you know, K, if Father came here?' K said. 'He might have. This gentleman could not be lying.'

The *panda* — his name was Vasudev and he wasn't such a bad man after all — had us where perhaps he wanted.

An hour later, we sat in a narrow dingy room with a skylight, staring at the yellowing leaf of a long ledger at the bottom of which stood the large bold signatures of my father. A date was mentioned below the signatures.

'Are these his signatures?' K asked.

'I think so. What about the date?'

'I think it is soon after your mother died.'

Muffled noises — the cry of a mule driver, quarrelling of a child, a radio — seeped softly into the room. The house was in a crowded locality. We had walked twenty minutes across a crisscross of undulating lanes, not unlike the lanes of Benaras. The light in the skylight began to falter. It would soon be night.

I mentioned the temple to Vasudev.

'Yes, that is a very famous place.'

'I know. I want to go there this evening.'

'This evening! No, not this evening. I took your father early in the morning. Everyone goes there in the morning. It will take you at least one hour.'

'My father went there, too?'

'Everyone goes there. The old and the cripple. The blind.'

'Where do you include me?' I said, with a laugh. I had a feeling it was after many hours that I had laughed. Vasudev was all apologies. How could Somji talk like that? Let his enemies be cripple and blind, and so on.

At night we ate with him. By now I had grown to like him. For his manners, and for something else as well. He provided a kind of security. Only now did I realize how insecure I had been all during the trip. He was no doubt doing all this for money but he was something — a man, an institution — one could fall back upon. For all I knew, his family had actually looked after ours for two hundred years. If the old man who died at the Lake could trust his priest to escort him to another world, I could surely trust Vasudev for a day or two.

In spite of Vasudev's prodding, we did not start early. Watched by a restless K, I dawdled over little rituals like trimming my nails, shaving twice. Finally we set out: Vasudev, K, and I. We descended the main street of the town watched by men on shop fronts and ladies in little green first-floor windows. Once again they reminded me of Benaras, of that particular street where Azizun and the two little girls lived. Men, their caps tilted at rakish angles, laughed like children, at nothing at all.

At the outskirts of the town a man, an acquaintance of Vasudev's fell in with us. He, too, he said, was going to the temple. A little later another joined us and then another until we were a little group. Gradually, I became aware of the knots of pilgrims scattered all over the plain, converging from every direction. The colours of their clothes, yellow, orange and maroon stood out against the green of the valley.

'Is there a special day today?' K asked Vasudev.

'Of course. It is a day for vows. Some come for new vows; others to thank for the old ones.'

'And their wishes get fulfilled?'

'It depends on their faith. Faith can move mountains, doctor sahib. Am I wrong? Please tell me if I am wrong. Modern people know so much more than we who have never stepped out of the village.'

We came now to a narrow stream with a wooden bridge. It was at this point that all those meandering pilgrims converged. There was a crowd of them on the bridge looking up and down the stream in either direction. The water fell in little cascades, clear and sparking. Vasudev asked me for a coin, shouted '*Jai* Krishna' and flipped it into the clear waters. Others followed him, each offering accompanied by a burst of '*Jai* Krishna'. I could see the coins scattered about the river bed. Some *mahant's* boy would no doubt climb in later and forage for them. The water must have been icy cold.

Beyond the stream, the plain narrowed rapidly, culmination in a steep pathway on which the pilgrims formed a steady upward moving escalator. A murmur, as though of the wind in a forest, arose in the distance. A young man, carrying a wizened old woman, her face a ball of white hair, asked for the time. It was almost noon.

The strange murmuring of the wind increased until a wail broke lose from somewhere and I realized that it was not wind at all but human voices that made the murmur. And presently, they came into view, the lepers that lined the path on either side. The first of them was a woman, her nose eaten away, leaving behind two holes. She sat hunched, in a low wooden trolley. She had a shrewd look in her yellow eyes. She was a curiosity until a sudden panic seized me that she was going to touch me and I jumped swiftly aside knocking in the process the young man with the piggyback mother. The man tottered a little but found his balance.

In a minute my curiosity turned into nightmare, although, neither Vasudev nor K seemed to take much notice of it. For Vasudev, it was nothing new and K, after all, was a doctor. The hard pavement now turned into a series of steps, rough and steep, hewn out of the hill itself. Wails and threats fell about us like ticker tape. I could not recall when I had seen such a grotesque collection of deformity and disease. How could these benign hills have produced so many lepers unless they came from the plains. A faint memory stirred at the back of my mind. What was it that Anuradha had said:

A hill lined with lepers. She had been drunk and half-asleep at the time and I had taken it to be the fragment of a nightmare. Could this be the hill she had in mind? 'There are a hundred steps like these,' Vasudev declared.

In another trolley sat a boy, his matchstick limbs wrapped around him. A young girl, her bright red tongue, like a snake's, darting about in her lipless mouth, grinned at me.

I turned to Vasudev, 'I had never seen so many lepers before,' I said weakly, as though conveying my admiration for a collection of rare painting.

Vasudev said nothing.

'Where do they come from?'

'From all over the country. They come to be cured.'

'Do they get cured?'

He evaded a reply.

'I suppose that depends on "faith" too,' I said.

'There is a tank behind the temple whose waters can cure.' Vasudev had been disbursing small change. K had handed him some of his own. Near the temple entrance, at the top of the steps, there was a wild melee of stumps, as the lepers tried their last chance at coercion.

We broke into a narrow corridor lined with flower sellers. Mountains of marigolds lay scattered in every form and shape — from petals to garlands. Here, too, our path was blocked by twenty tattooed arms, rather like the arms of brokers in the Stock Exchange; each holding a leaf cup of flowers. Vasudev bought a cup. K, too, bought one. The marigolds reminded me of the astrologer at the carnival.

On the vast stone platform of the temple I could breathe again.

'You were looking choked back there,' said K.

'It *was* bad, you'll admit.'

'Where to, now?'

'I don't know.'

After a moment's hesitation, we let the stream of people carry us. In the distance I could see another entrance. It was made of marble. In the middle of it hung a bronze bell which everyone jumped and clanged. I wondered why it had been placed so high. Children were raised on shoulders so they could ring it. It was while I was watching the bell, wondering what we were to do after we had passed under it, that someone said in English, 'Come this way, please.'

It was a short, stocky, middle-aged man who had spoken. He had closely cropped grey hair and light eyes like Leela Sabnis. Judging by his accent he might have been from around Bombay, too. He could have been a retired civil servant.

All three of us stepped out of the crowd expecting a further explanation. None, however, was offered. Without a word he led us to the back of the main temple. We came to a two-storeyed building, recently white-washed, gleaming in the sun. There was a *dharmashala* on the ground floor. Three men sat on cot smoking from a hukka. We crossed the *dharmashala,* emerged in the open and started to climb a spiral staircase which, for some reason, had been left unpainted. The others climbed easily, I stumbled a little. The steps were steep and I had begun to feel the cumulated exhaustion of the previous week. On a landing above, K came to a halt. Silent and very still, one hand shading his eyes against the sun, he stared at whatever it was that lay in the distance. Presently, I joined him. Before us, in the dazzling light, across a narrow valley loomed the mountain that we had seen from the lake two nights earlier. It must have been hidden from view by the flank of the hill on which the temple stood. It seemed close enough to be within an hour's walk although, in fact, it must have been much farther. The narrow strip of the intervening valley was a brilliant green dotted with several pinnacled Buddhist shrines. Before each shrine tall poles flew their numerous flags. The silence was total.

We crossed another yard before entering a small room. The room was familiar. There were mats on the floor and a pitcher of water. There were the familiar coloured glass ventilators. The sun, percolating through them, threw a collage of lights on the floor. In the middle of this sat Gargi. Our guide bowed, did his *namaskar*, and departed. Gargi walked briskly over to where we stood and took my hand. 'This *is* a surprise,' I said, breathless, fumbling for words. 'What are *you* doing here?'

Gargi smiled her beautiful, enigmatic smile, led us to the cushions near the windows and settled us all down as though nothing could have been more natural than this visit. I wondered what Vasudev made of the whole thing. I whispered to him, 'She is a friend of mine. She cannot hear or speak but she can read lips.'

'I know. I know,' he whispered back.

'How do you know?'

'Everyone knows about her.' His voice was subdued and full of awe. 'I think I should go away,' he continued. 'I did not know you were coming here.' He got up. I took his hand and tried to pull him down. He freed himself, also did *namaskar* to Gargi and departed.

Gargi watched us amiably while we conducted this exchange. Once again the plump rosy face, the intelligent understanding eyes, evoked in me the overwhelming compulsion to talk and talk and talk. I could never understand why she had that effect on me. And so over the next half hour I talked without a break: of my illness, of our travels. I tried to talk about Anuradha but the pain was too great and I gave up. If I had known she was here, I said, I would have written to her in advance.

'She must have known we were coming,' interrupted K. 'Or, why the guide.'

'Were you expecting us?' I asked Gargi.

She did not answer.

So once again, I was silenced by the intrusion of the unknown. Tea was brought in tall steel tumblers. I recognized the girl who had been Gargi's companion in Benaras. She recognized me, too, and smiled. We drank the tea in silence. It was a neat cosy corner. At Gargi's back were a series of narrow windows, their panels brightly painted. The windows were open and looked over the same valley, the same Buddhist shrines with their poles of fluttering flags. A

Sri Chakra hung on the wall facing me. Belatedly, I thought of introducing K. 'This is Dr. Kashyap. He saved my life.'

K shifted uncomfortably, a rare thing for him, and once again the thought crossed my mind that he was aware of things about which I did not know.

For the moment, though, I was too relieved to have found Gargi to worry much about other things. I realized now, all said and done, how edgy I had been all these days, like a man in a maze who, though on the right track, is apprehensive of what he might find at the centre of it. Gargi's plump pink face was nothing if not reassuring. And once again, I felt, a I had felt many times before that she was the only one who understood.

I did not talk to her about the shares because I did not think she would know about them. There had to be someone else on the precincts who would be accounting for such things. Mr. Thapar had been told as much by the secretary of temple. I found myself describing to her the lake, the glacier, the old man and his grandson. I talked at such lengths that she must have wondered what had come over me.

'Now, what could be the significance of it?' I asked.

I stared at Gargi as though I expected her to reply. When she didn't, I added, 'I suppose it had significance for the old man who believed in it.'

'Didn't you find the boy amazing, though?' I asked K.

'He reminded me of you when you were a boy,' said K.

'You must be joking.'

'It is hard to believe but he did remind me of you. Something happened to you when your mother died.'

I kept quiet, in a way dreading what he might say. 'I think you lost your nerve,' K said.

Gargi had been watching us. I knew she had understood every word that had been spoken. It was amazing how she could make people talk. She had made even K open up. Said he, 'But, all in all, it is not death but life that you are bothered about. Or, so I think. You are like your father. He also wanted to know if there was a First Cause.'

'Behind death?'

'Behind life. In life.'

'Depends upon what side of the coin you are looking.'

'There is a profound difference in the two sides,' K said.

After a moment's silence he continued, 'Life to your father was the expression of a will, but he wanted to know "whose will". I think you know all this.'

'I do, but carry on.'

'Was it his will, he wanted to know, or a divine will — the will of the First Cause? He knew enough to realize that it could not be his will alone. But he did not have the evidence to believe that there was a divine will. So he could not make up his mind.'

'And slipped into melancholia?'

'Perhaps.'

I wondered what had made us slip into such an odd discussion in this, of all places. It was as though in Bombay all these years we had never had the time. Gargi, who realized that our discussion had ended, now suggested by a gesture that we should rest. There were mats lying scattered about along the walls of the room. We lay down obediently. I realized how tired I was and wondered if exhaustion could bring on a heart attack as K had warned. Then I fell asleep and dreamt the same old dream — of the plane and the mountain and the terrifying crash. I had not until my illness believed people when they talked of their recurrent nightmares. For me it was not a nightmare any more but a depressing chore; a kind of a punishment, something like the fatigue that soldiers are sentenced to.

I woke up to the tinkling of bells. It wasn't bells, though, but utensils. Lunch had been brought for us by the same stocky grey-haired man. K was already seated and was calling my name.

Dazed by the dream, I stumbled towards the meal which had been laid in the middle of the room. Gargi watched me curiously as I settled down. It was as though she saw something in my face which had not been there before. Instead of eating, I found myself relating the dream to her and telling her how sick I was of dreaming it over and over again, like having to repeatedly watch a bad movie against one's will. Gargi smiled, took out her pad and 'Your food is getting cold' she wrote. 'You will not have this dream again if you don't want to.'

After lunch, Gargi made paans for everybody. I wondered how to proceed about the mystery of the shares. Would she know? What would she say?

In the event, it was K, of all people, who took up the unravelling of it. After some hesitation he had come to a decision. He addressed Gargi. He spoke slowly so she would understand him.

'I did not save Som, as he mentioned some time back. In fact, by my understanding he was as good as dead when Anuradha came to see him the evening of his attack. This is important. Do you understand me?'

Gargi nodded. K took time organizing the next set of thoughts.

'Now, the night before we started on this journey Anuradha spoke to me on phone. She told me the following. She said from Som's sick-bed she came to you. She told you what I had told her. That there was no hope for Som. She begged you to save him. You laughed her away, saying he was in good hands and what could you do that the doctors could not. You said you could not perform miracles. Anuradha persisted, wept, begged and threatened. She said to you she could not live without Som and she would eat poison if something happened to him. She said your father had given Aftab his eyesight so why could you not save Som's life. She said she would not go home until you did something for Som.'

There was another pause. Gargi had been listening carefully, attentively, trying not to miss anything he said. 'Is all this correct?' K asked her.

Gargi made no response. K repeated the question. Gargi gave him her charming smile.

K stared out of the windows. I could see his mind working, trying to tackle the question another way. 'I am a medical doctor. I do not believe in things in which Anuradha believes. But I know for a fact that Som had no chance whatsoever and I want to know: did you save him? Anuradha says you did. And in return for what you did, she says, you made her promise that she would give up Som. For ever. That to her, Som would be dead, either way. Is this true? Please tell me.'

There was great intensity in his question. It affected me. For a moment it affected Gargi as well. She took out a pad from under the mat and wrote out a few words. 'I cannot tell you what you want to know,' the note said.

I could see the disappointment in K's face. He carried on with his precise lawyer-like presentation. 'Anyway,' he said, 'there is another thing. At the end of whatever it was that you did, as a gift for the gods, Anuradha left with you all her jewellery and a package of shares that this foolish man has been hunting for. That, I understand, was all the wealth that she had at the time.'

Gargi wrote out her reply readily enough. After reading it K passed it on to me. 'I have a package. I have been asked by the Secretary of the temple to hand it over to you. I do not know what it contains. I can give it to you tomorrow if you come in the morning.'

I did not know what to make of what I had heard. For a second I thought K had made up the story on the spur of the moment. Except that it was a very odd story to cook up. Moreover, the matter, all said and done, was serious. Exchanges had obviously taken place between K and Anuradha; even between K and Geeta who, perhaps, had received information, in turn, from Anuradha. It really was ironic that both my wife and my mistress should gang up against me. Gargi's note, of course, did not admit anything, which left the matter doubtful.

There was a businesslike finality about Gargi's note. It left little room for discussion. Her muteness which had always brought forth such streams of loquacity from me, now left me tongue-tied. Here was this package. I could take it or leave it. She was going to offer me neither explanation nor advice. I had the confused feeling that I was being put on a hook and she was going to do nothing to get me off.

Yet, I did try to seek explanations but met with the same enigmatic smile that had earlier greeted K. One could believe that this happened, that a miracle took place or one need not believe it. Gargi did not seem to mind either way.

Minutes passed in silence. After a decline during the afternoon the bustle in the precincts of the temple was again on the increase. Suddenly, the idea of visiting the deity entered my head and I mentioned it to Gargi. She nodded, rang a tiny bell. The guide appeared again. He seemed to understand what we wanted. We took leave of Gargi.

As we went down the spiral staircase I noticed the declining sun at the far end of the valley. The shadows of the Tibetan poles slanted the other way. Beyond, on the mountain peak, the light had already died. The silence was unbroken.

'There is no deity as such in this temple,' our guide explained. 'Only a flame.'

'A flame?'

'These were volcanic mountains at one time. A jet of natural gas has burnt in the sanctum of this temple at least for a thousand years.'

'And that is your deity?'

'Yes.'

The crowds were still thin. We were ushered into a circular chamber with a rockfloor. In the centre of the floor shot a dazzling blue flame. It was taller than me and burnt quietly. I now realized that it was only the authority of our guide that had enabled us to come so close to it. The pilgrims watched it from a distance of more than fifty feet.

We looked at it in wonder. This, then, was Krishna, was it? The circular chamber reminded me of another place but I could not immediately recall it. And then the thought crossed my mind that if this was God and this was *all* that was God and if there was no proof that a miracle saved me, then, I was going to take the shares the following morning. And not just the shares. Kneeling beside that fantastic flame, my heart bursting with sorrow and my old demented love for Anuradha, I vowed I was going to reverse the whole thing: I was going to get the shares *and* Anuradha. No half-assed rigmarole was going to keep us apart.

We emerged at last on the steps of the temple and were led through the leper's guard. On the narrow bridge our guide bid us good bye.

~

That night we sat in Vasudev's house. My spirits were down. I felt somehow defeated. Even physically I felt feebler than I had at any time during the trip. We sat on cots, wrapped in quilts. K smoked.

'What's the matter?' he said, turning towards me.

'It's too complicated.'

'What is it?'

'I was thinking about what you told Gargi. I don't believe it. And if I do, I can't get over the fact that Anuradha should give me up for a gimmick like that.'

'What gimmick?'

'This thing that Gargi presumably did the night I had my attack. And Anuradha promising to give me up and the gift of the shares to Krishna etc. etc.'

'Why do you think it was a gimmick?'

'What else should one think? What do you think?'

K smoked in silence. He finished smoking, extinguished the stub against the floor and flipped it out of the doorway. Without looking at me he said, 'It may not have been a gimmick, you know.' 'It need not have been a gimmick,' he repeated, turning towards me. 'As I told Gargi, as far as I was concerned, I had entirely given you up that night you had your attack.'

'So?'

'You don't understand. There are cases where a doctor feels the patient has a chance, howsoever small. There are other cases where he knows the patient has *no* chance whatsoever.

'One in a million? In ten million?'

'You are splitting hairs. You were ninety-nine per cent dead that night. The balance one per cent would have died within twenty four hours. Anuradha came there that night. I told her you had no chance.'

I realized now that I was fidgety and irritated. Maybe it was K, or what he was saying, that was working on me. Maybe it was the medicine that I had just taken.

'So you think a miracle took place?'

'I don't know.'

'Why can't you decide?'

'It is you who have to make up your mind. And there is no need to lose your temper.'

'I am sorry,' I said. And that was the end of our discussion. Neither of us probably wanted to get too involved with it.

A little later, K fell asleep. I sat by myself, staring at the flame of the candle. It was unnaturally still, as though carved out of stone. There was the outer yellow ring growing lighter as it moved inwards, until it melted into the little blue drops of pure heat at the core. Maybe, this flame and that other flame in the temple were somehow connected, as all fire was connected. Its perfect stillness could hypnotize. I had heard of people who, staring into such flames, had enjoyed the Eternal Bliss. It was always spelt in capitals.

Others had discovered their Oneness (another capital-prone word) with the Brahma. A man I once travelled with — one of the most sophisticated I have ever met — claimed he had seen in such a flame his previous incarnations. He had been a teacher, a butcher, a dancing girl, he said.

This little flame of mine, however, yielded nothing beyond an ounce of tranquillity which, of course, was not to be laughed at. And, then, through the tranquillity, came the old sorrow. It had always been like that. 'What do you know of sorrow,' Aftab had once said. I did not know about his definition of sorrow. Just because one did not brood around in grim havelis did not mean one was unacquainted with sorrow.

Staring at the little flame I was back in the circular chamber of the temple where the man-high flame burnt. It reminded me. I knew now, of that cave of Ajanta on which I had felt the first onslaught of the voids. What could be a greater void than a void in which a flame consumed all.

Damn, I said. Damn.

I was still saying 'Damn' and 'Damn' when I went to sleep. I dreamt that I was back in Lal Haveli. I saw lamps everywhere. A wedding was on. Aftab said Anuradha was getting married. 'But she is married to me,' I cried. He laughed. Then the lights were gone. Aftab and I sat in a room that I had never seen before and played chess. He said, 'Can you fly? Like a bird?' I said yes. We went up numerous stairs. 'You must jump from here.' Aftab said. And he pushed me.

As I fell through the air I awoke. My heart was palpitating. I was drenched in sweat. I considered awakening K but thought better of it. I took a strong tranquillizer. I didn't want any more dreams, for God's sake. But I had them anyway. I dreamt that I was crying. I sat alone and cried in my house in Bombay. Aftab came in and said. 'It is very hot outside. Why not let the hot air dry your tears.' And then he was chasing me down the beach and in a narrow Benaras lane. There were people with him carrying long knives, the ones they used for the slaughter of goats. There was people in the side lanes as well, Aftab's friends, ready to kill me as they would kill a dog. I dashed into a house and discovered it was the Lal Haveli. I was crying for help. I ran up flights of stairs. I could feel the pounding of feet behind me. On the landing, I ran into Gargi who put her arm around me and pressed her thighs against mine.

When I awoke it was still dark. I did not feel rested. I felt more exhausted than I had during the whole trip. Very soon, I knew, K would be awake and I would have to tell him if we were going back to the temple. I lay next to a window with narrow slats. I reached out and opened one of them. A fine mist laced with wood-smoke filtered in. Lying in bed, wrapped in my sleeping bag, I could see a little distance into the swirling fog. It soothed my tired eyes, cleared my brain a bit. I wondered where one went from there, from that room, that hillside.

Was this it, then? The terminus? The last of the labyrinth? A tobacco-stained house; a register with my father's signature; a temple on a hill; flags in the wind; a deaf-mute priestess; hints of a miracle? Was it this that I had wanted all my life? Was this the answer to the relentless chant 'I want, I want.' Why was it so unsatisfying? Or, may be, the labyrinth hadn't ended. Something else lay ahead, something more fundamental than a miracle, something I would know only if I took the shares from Gargi. If God existed, if a miracle had taken place, and now if I walked off with the shares — and with Anuradha — I should perhaps die.

That was a hell of a thought to be burdened with but I didn't think I had a choice. All I knew was that I wasn't prepared to give up Anuradha on these grounds.

The fog moved in cones and circles and curlicues and watching it, I fell asleep again.

When I next awoke the sun was high. K stood by the door, smoking. The fog was gone. Vasudev brought us tea laced with cinnamon. Half-way through the tea, I said to K, 'I think we shall go back to the temple, after all.' He didn't answer. After an interval, he said, 'You go there alone. I will not be accompanying you.'

Vasudev, who had been listening to the little exchange, now pitched in. 'Forgive me for putting my head where I should not,' he said. 'But I am also your humble servant and must have my say.'

We turned to look at him.

'Somji is unhappy. I do not want him to be unhappy. I do not know what the difficulty is but I think Somji should do exactly what Gargi Mata tells him.'

'But Gargi Mata does not say a thing. Nothing at all.' I could hear the frustration in my voice.

'In that case you should ask her,' said Vasudev.

He had a point.

~

So I covered the last bit of that journey alone. Gargi was there, sitting on a cot, out on the courtyard facing the Tibetan shrines, sunning herself. I thought of my dream about her and wondered what it meant.

'I have come for the package,' I said. 'I am sorry the doctor could not come,' I added irrelevantly.

She did not hesitate, or ponder, or look grave as I had imagined but went inside and quickly returned with a sealed cloth bundle, a bit like the parcels carried around by postmen. Gargi handed it to me with her usual smile.

I took the package. 'Let us sit down,' I said gesturing towards the cot. 'I want to ask you something.' We sat down. I said, 'I think I can be honest with you. I think you will understand what I am going to say. I can do without these shares if I find a reason to do so. I had bought them because I had a score to settle with Aftab and Anuradha. I didn't like the way Anuradha ditched me after the illness. But, after what K said yesterday, I have become confused. Did Anuradha and you do something to save me when I had that heart attack? If so, you must tell me. You must advise me what to do.'

Gargi looked as though expecting me to go on. If she remains mum, I said to myself, if she remains mum, by God, I am going to walk off with these shares.

Just then she wrote something on her pad. 'There is no harm in believing that God exists,' the note said. She had a neat precise hand.

So I was back with Pascal! I said, 'It is easier to believe that He does not exist. It is more convenient that way.'

Gargi nodded, smiled.

'No, don't misunderstand me. I *want* to know. Probably, I *want* to believe. But one can't order belief. I must have evidence. You see what I mean? I cannot give up Anuradha, you know that. In the absence of evidence I intend to challenge the whole thing: I want to take not only these shares but also Anuradha. It scares me but I have no choice.'

Gargi laughed, then wrote on her pad, 'God does not work in this simple manner, God does not seek revenge. Man's...'

She faltered, handed me the pad and went inside. She came back with a heavy book. It was a Hindi-English dictionary. She completed the sentence. 'Man's vanity (*ahankar*) brings him revenge enough.'

I looked at the note for a long time. Gargi got me tea. I studied the note as though it were a hieroglyph, a coded instruction to a mysterious destination. Finally, I said to Gargi: 'I want to assure you I am not vain. I am not arrogant. I am curious. I want to know. May be over-curious but not vain. So, I'll take these shares with me.'

Gargi wrote again: 'We are all children trying to reach up to a crack in the door to peep into a room.'

She laughed as she handed the note to me. 'You mean I am like a little child.' She laughed again. 'As for Anuradha,' I repeated, in an unsteady voice, 'as for her I can't give her up on these... flimsy grounds. I can't live without her. You should know that.'

She smiled, patted my cheek, made a gesture as of a blessing. On an impulse I bent down and touched her feet. Then I left.

I came slowly down the stairs feeling apprehensive as though the package was going to explode any minute. Gradually, my apprehension faded away.

It was a mild afternoon. The sky was sharp blue and cloudless. Beyond the lepers the valley was a soothing green. The mountain range glowed in the sun. I crossed the bridge, then walked a little way up the stream. The water shimmered in the sunlight. It gurgled so one could hear nothing else. I touched the water. It was extremely cold. It might have been snowing that morning.

I lay down by the stream, the bundle under my head. Above me, the vast canopy of the sky suddenly appeared as though I had never seen it before. I was reminded of Prince Andrew, knocked down like a dummy without firing a shot. He had imagined himself to be ambitious. He had hoped Austerlitz would do for him what Toulon had done for the Bonaparte. Lying in the mud, canon balls flying over him, he had stared at the vast cosmic impersonal dome of the sky and had wondered: 'My God, where have I been all these years. Why had I never looked at the sky before.'

'We are like children trying to reach up to a crack in the door to peep into a room,' Gargi had said. I wished she had elaborated. I wished she had *told* me what lay in the room. Maybe she did not know herself. Maybe, it was better she did not tell me. Maybe I would not have believed even if she *had* told me. One had probably to rise up to the crack by oneself.

I got up, gathered my package, and started to climb down.

4

It was raining. The overcast gave an idea of dusk before it was dusk. There was little activity in the streets around Lal Haveli.

Aftab and I sat on the porch near the fountain. It was the first time we had sat there. Without Anuradha and Azizun, the Blue

Room could not perhaps be entered. There was no thunder from the silent sky but rain poured without a break. There would soon be another birthday of God. Tarakki sat at the far end, his eyes wide in wonder as though seeing rain for the first time. Aftab saw my glance.

'Tarakki waits for the snakes to come out,' he said.

'Whatever for?'

'You will see for yourself. Some poor snake is bound to come along.'

We went back to silence. Somewhere in the haveli Azizun carried on her *riyaz*. 'The rain has stirred something in her.' Aftab said. 'It does the same thing to her every year.' Anuradha was probably in her room dressing for the evening. I did not remember an instance when she had not dressed for the evening. I thought of the times I had had her in the middle of her dressing. A feeling of frustration grew upon me. I said, 'I have bought the control of your company, Aftab.' 'Oh!' he said after a long pause, his eyes glancing in the middle distance. He did not seem surprised. 'It was possible some such thing would happen.' In the corner of my eye I caught a brown and yellow splash. A snake struggled in the trough of a drain pipe fighting the cascade of water. Tarakki was upon it in a flash. He whirled it holding it by the tail, then, with one violent heave, smashed its head against the fountain. Little splinters of something flew out of the snake's head. The incident took a couple of seconds. 'Good God,' I said, fighting back a fit of retching.

Aftab quietly shook his head.

'That was horrible,' I said, feeling a new indignation.

'Horror is a part of life,' Aftab said. 'Perhaps the greater part.'

~

We sat in a darkened Blue Room. The power had gone off. Azizun's *riyaz* had ended. I had not yet seen Anuradha even though I had been at Lal Haveli for several hours.

Aftab offered me his cigarettes which I turned down. 'You have been to the hills, haven't you?' he inquired.

'How did you know?'

He kept quiet, lit a cigarette. I watched him smoke, 'I had hoped you would not come back,' he said.

'Oh!'

'I had hoped you would die climbing those rocks.'

'I nearly did.'

'Nearly is never the same thing.'

'Are you disappointed?'

'Very much. Unfortunately, I like you. I wish you had left us alone. Anuradha and I need each other.'

'So you imagine. You treat her worse than you treat that Azizun girl.'

'That is what you think. I told you, you are different. You don't understand us. You work by logic. By your brain. You are proud of your education or what you consider education. There is an understanding that only suffering and humiliation bring. Anuradha has that. Even I have a bit of it. You are empty of that understanding.'

'I wish you would stop lecturing me and do something about the electricity.'

'That is not in my hand,' he chuckled.

Time passed. It was still raining. There was still no electricity. Tarakki had come and put a lantern between us.

'So you have our company,' Aftab said.

'Yes.'

'And you want Anuradha now?'

'Yes.'

'You learnt nothing in the mountains.'

'Is that a question?'

'No.'

'Shall I explain?'

'No.'

I started to speak, say something caustic. I had had enough of this polite exchange. I was interrupted by what sounded like a sob. Like the cry of an animal in great pain which it could no longer bear. I leaned forward and there, sure enough, in the yellow light of the lantern, Aftab wept. After that initial wail he cried in silence. Tears welled inside his goggles and spilled over on to his cheeks, his lips, his throat. He made no attempt to dry them.

Still crying, he got up. 'Good night,' he whispered through his tears.

'Good night,' I said. 'I want to see Anuradha before I go.'

'I'll send her,' he said.

I sat alone smoking, feeling very tense. Anuradha was certainly taking her time. I looked around restlessly. That room had never been fully lighted. There were objects in it that I might have seen just as I could not imagine all the strange happenings, happy, sad, and cruel, that must have occurred within its four walls.

At the far end, it was completely dark. I could see neither the arch nor the broken fountain. Against the stone of the courtyard the rain beat harder than ever. Minutes passed without Anuradha making an appearance. My tension grew. I took a few steps towards the courtyard, stumbled against a hump in the carpet and returned to the sofa. It was true one could lose one's way in the maze of that haveli.

Finally, I heard steps, someone running across the courtyard. Anuradha came in through the arch wiping her face with her sari. I rushed towards her, took her hands in mine. I wanted to say something but my voice choked. She tried to free her hands but I wouldn't let her go.

'I love you,' I said at last.

'You must go away now.' There was an unfamiliar urgency in her voice.

'You must come with me,' I said.

'Come with you? You talk like a child. But you must go away. Return to the hotel. Go back by the morning flight.'

'Come with me to the hotel. Stay with me the night. Tomorrow we shall return to Bombay.'

'You don't understand. You don't know these people. Things could happen to you in this haveli and no one would ever know.'

'I shall return Aftab his shares.'

'That is not the point. It is not a question of the shares.'

I tried to argue. She put her hand on my mouth. 'Don't argue. Go away now and we might still have a chance. I have called a taxi for you.'

There was the sound of a car moving to the front of the building. 'Go away now,' she said pushing me towards the door. Maybe she was right. Maybe she needed time to handle Aftab Rai.

'I'll go now,' I said. 'But I'll come back in the morning. Tell Aftab I'll give him back his shares.'

'Good bye.'

When I went back the next morning it was still raining. Along the *ghats,* a crowd of drenched singing dancing people, rain streaming down their faces, had blocked our taxi for an hour. Aftab met me in the Blue Room. He looked haggard. He wore the same clothes in which I had left him the previous night. He had not shaved and it did not look as though he had slept.

'You have come to see Anuradha?' he said with a half-smile.

I nodded.

'Well, she has disappeared.'

'Disappeared where?'

'If I knew she would not be considered disappeared. She went to the temple last night for Janmashtami and she hasn't come back.'

'It was Janmashtami last night?'

'Yes.'

Krishna! I thought, Krishna again. There was something else, though. Why had she not made a mention of it to me?

'How did she go to the temple.'

'Tarakki dropped her.'

'I don't believe you,' I said trying to control my rage and my despair.

Aftab shrugged.

'If you don't mind I am going to inform the police.'

'As you like,' he said, getting up.

5

From where I sit I can see the line of shimmering surf. The moon is high. To my left lies little mound where honeymooning couples pose to have their pictures taken. Somewhere beyond the mound, along the curve of the beach, I had walked with my father that day after our visit to Elephanta.

Geeta sleeps next door. The children, too, are home for vacation. It is a quiet, restful, perfect life. But I cannot sleep and, at times, I go out on the beach and cradled by the roar of the sea I cry to the stars.

Months have passed but there is no news of Anuradha. I did go to the police in Benaras and registered a case. Aftab sat in silence while they searched his haveli. They found nothing except a bit of her antique clothing. 'It is true,' said a tired superintendent, 'it is true things could happen in this haveli without leaving a trace. But we cannot demolish the whole place. We cannot take it apart.' Tarakki's evidence that he had dropped her at the temple, held. Anuradha's pictures were flashed to every police station in the country.

I whistle for Banjo. He creeps out from under the bed, stretches himself, hind legs first then the fore legs. 'How about a stroll, old man?' Somehow he understands this — always has — and pricks up his ears. I open the rosewood cabinet, pick out my grandfather's gun, tuck it in my trousers. We step out.

The sand is cool to my bare feet. I roll up my trousers an inch or two and we make slowly for the mound. It stands in the moonlight like a mutilated breast. Some nights ago, I thought I had seen the lean, hungry face of Tarakki lurking in its shadows, his eyes towards my house. At the time I had dismissed it as a hallucination.

We climb the mound and sit down. The gun makes it difficult for me to sit properly. I adjust the butt until the barrel settles comfortably against my belly like a secret limb. Grandfather's ideas are not without their use.

The roar of the sea is loud here. A plane goes by overhead, a jumbo, slow and graceful, its wings unfurled. I see its landing lights go on and off but, because of the crashing surf, I cannot hear the jets. I remember how my father had stood staring up at such blinking lights that evening fifteen years ago. And, I remember how I had patronized him that night. 'But surely you *want* to understand, Som,' my father had said, looking curiously into my face.

Last night I dreamt again of Aftab's haveli, its arches and silent courtyards and the sarcophagus of green marble. Wandering through the mazes the police had come back to it, again and again, but they could not touch it, dared not touch it. I dreamt I stood near the sarcophagus and, while I stood, it changed into the bar of the Intercontinental, its brass-work gleaming through the mist of the dream. A drugged Aftab Rai leaned against the railing. Someone said, 'He is dead. He is dead.' Just then Aftab's corpse stretched out its hand and caught me by the wrist. I woke up, shaken.

Some time back I received a letter from Aftab. It was unstamped and unsigned but I could recognize the large, unsteady hand. The moon is bright but not bright enough for me to read it here. But I have read it many times before and, by and large, I know its incoherent contents.

'For me now,' he writes, 'all is desolation...' take hold I tell myself... "take hold Aftab Rai, you can live without her"... but I cannot live without her... endlessly, I walk the mazes... night turns into day... day into night... I knock my head against walls... cry out my love for her... she does not listen... I am finished... I had liked you... I had let a snake enter my home... she thought she would handle you... she came that night from Bombay and said you were dying... the secret of her love written on her face... I was happy you were dying... she went across the river... spoke of the night many years ago... when she cut her wrists... told me you will never... never put your treacherous foot in Lal Haveli... but I knew... she knew... if she was proven wrong... if you ever returned... you would pay heavily... why did you return... how I hate you... curse you... you escaped to the hotel that night... but how long... your time will come... while you live you will rot... when dead you shall not find peace... from one graveyard to another you will wander... a million years.'

I light a cigarette.

Aftab's letter explains nothing beyond confirming that it was indeed Tarakki whom I saw the other night. I must now at all times be ready to receive Aftab's emissary. Like a curse, I carry my grandfather's gun wherever I go.

In place of Anuradha, of Gargi, we now only have this terrible, terrible, hatred in common. And where is Anuradha?

Anuradha, listen. Listen to me wherever you are. Is there a God where you are? Have you met Him? Does He have a face? Does He speak? Does He hear? Does He understands the language that we speak? Anuradha, if there is a God and if you have met Him and if He is willing to listen, then, Anuradha, my soul, tell Him, tell this God, to have mercy upon me. Tell Him I am weary. Of so many fears; so much doubting. Of this dark earth and these empty heavens. Plead for me, Anuradha. He will listen to you.

I marvel at the strange mad thoughts that at times carom around my skull. Are they harbingers, the pilot-escort, of melancholia? Of insanity? Faith? You never know what is the pilot-escort of what.

Of my companies, the less said the better. Mr. Thapar struggles day and night to put them back on the rails. If anyone can straighten them out he can. I pitch in whenever required. It is a big mess.

~

I bury the half-smoked cigarette in sand and stand up. Banjo follows suit. Another liner goes by with a great roar. It comes in dangerously low, so low that I can see the bright port-holes and the colours of British Airways. As I approach the house, the figure of a woman appears at the window of my room. Geeta, after all, is not asleep. She watches me as I wipe my shoes on the door-mat. There is something that Aftab wrote about her that I forgot. Somewhere amidst those broken words he writes: 'Geeta knew.' But what did she know? When did they meet? Did he write?

Geeta watches me as I come in. I pull out the revolver, take a step towards the cabinet, then turn around and put it casually to my temple. She steps forward, alarmed, unbelieving. 'Don't,' she whispers. I laugh, pull the gun away, put it on 'safety' and dump it in the cabinet. Geeta puts her hand on my arm. In her nightie and dressing gown she looks good, very good. 'Som...' she begins. I shake my head slowly, from side to side, a long time, as though I had a headache. 'Som...,' she repeats, shaking me gently as though rousing a man from sleep. I hold up a weary arm, the palm facing her, like a traffic policeman. I hope she understands.

❑❑❑

GLOSSARY

Aarati	A Hindu ritual of worship in praise of deity.
Angithi	Fireplace, brazier.
Bhang	Intoxicant.
Bhul-bhulaiyan	A maze; labyrinth.
Chaat	A mix of highly spiced potatoes, flour fritters topped with a thick sauce of chillies, black salt and tamarind.
Chaatwalahs	Seller of *chaat.*
Chikan	A style of fine and delicate embroidery.
Chimtas	Tongs.
Choli	Blouse.
Chowk	A Hindi word for square or crossroads.
Churidar	Tight fitting pyjamas commonly worn by both men and women in the Indian sub-continent.
Cowrie	Till the mid-20th century, the lowest unit of currency in India.
Dharamshala	Shelter or a rest house, traditionally for pilgrims.
Fana	Death or destruction.
Gajra	A small flower garland worn by women either around their wrist or woven into the hair.
Garara	Loose pyjamas worn by women.
Ghat	A level place on the edge of a river where Hindus cremate their dead.
Ghunghrus	Small metallic bells strung together to form an anklet and used by classical dancers.
Jaimal	Garland of flowers.
Kalash	Pinnacle of a temple.
Kamiz	A long shirt worn by many people in the Indian sub-continent, typically with a *salwar.*

Kirtan	Devotional singing.
Lokalok	Literally, this world and not-this-world.
Lungi	Broad piece of cloth wrapped around the waist which serves as a sleeping pyjama, a swimming or bathing suit.
Mahant	An ascetic, who is the head of a temple or monastery.
Mallah	Boatman.
Mehndi	Henna.
Mantra jap	Repeated recitation of a mantra (a group of words chanted as a prayer).
Motia	A type of white flower.
Mul	Muslin.
Namaskar	Traditional form of greeting with folded hands in Indian sub-continent.
Paandan	Box in which betel leaves and other ingredients for rolling it are kept.
Pajeb	Anklet.
Palki	Palanquin.
Panda	Priests or half priests usually found at religious places.
Prasad	Something edible, first offered to a deity and then distributed amongst followers.
Rangoli	Traditional Indian decoration and patterns made on the floor usually with coloured ground rice, particularly during festivals.
Rehris	Cart used by roadside vendors to display and sell their wares.
Riyaz	Practice especially of singing and dancing.
Shakti	Strength; the female principle of divine energy, especially when personified as the supreme deity.
Shamianas	Pavilions, canopy.
Shrimanji	Mister.
Sowars	Here it refers to horse-mounted soldiers.
Taluqdars	Landowners.